OSPREY COMBAT AIRCRAFT • 84

F-105 THUNDERCHIEF UNITS OF THE VIETNAM WAR

SERIES EDITOR: TONY HOLMES

OSPREY COMBAT AIRCRAFT • 84

F-105 THUNDERCHIEF UNITS OF THE VIETNAM WAR

PETER E DAVIES

OSPREY
PUBLISHING

Front cover
Vice Wing Commander of the 388th Tactical Fighter Wing (TFW) Col Jacksel Broughton led a flak suppression flight of four 354th Tactical Fighter Squadron (TFS) F-105Ds against railway marshalling yard targets between Viet Tri and Phu Tho, in North Vietnam, on 11 July 1967. Each pilot hit a separate gun emplacement, with Col Broughton (in his personal F-105D 62-4338 *Alice's Joy*) making the last attack in a 40-degree dive at military power from 12,000 ft seconds after the others. Aiming for a cluster of trans-shipment buildings each side of the railway lines at the eastern end of the marshalling yard, he released the six M117 750-lb bombs on his centreline rack at 4000 ft. All of his weapons were on target, the latter including two major anti-aircraft emplacements – one consisting of a ring of 85 mm guns and a second with massive 100 mm weapons. Both sites fired at him as he hurtled towards them. 'I think they used their entire daily quota of ammunition on me', Broughton recounted after the mission. Like the rest of the flight, he escaped unscathed.

In addition to the heavy guns, the Thunderchiefs had destroyed 35 railway trucks, cut the track in a dozen places and demolished several large storage buildings.

Flak suppression was one of the most dangerous missions flown by F-105 units in Vietnam, pilots seeking to provoke AAA batteries into action so that they could then target them just ahead of the main strike force. Although the F-105 combat wings attained a commendably low loss rate of 1.6 aircraft per 1000 sorties up to the final months of 1967, the sheer quantity of missions meant that a staggering 330 Thunderchiefs had been lost in action by that time, and only 367 of the original 833 production F-105D/Fs remained in service by August 1968 (*Cover Artwork by Gareth Hector using a model supplied by Milviz*)

First published in Great Britain in 2010 by Osprey Publishing
Midland House, West Way, Botley, Oxford, OX2 0PH
44-02 23rd St, Suite 219, Long Island City, New York, 11101
E-mail; info@ospreypublishing.com

Print ISBN 978 1 84603 492 3
PDF e-book ISBN 978 1 84908 255 6

Edited by Tony Holmes
Page design by Tony Truscott
Cover Artwork by Gareth Hector using a model supplied by Milviz
Aircraft Profiles by Jim Laurier
Index by Alan Thatcher
Originated by PDQ Digital Media Solutions, Suffolk, UK
Printed in China through Bookbuilders

10 11 12 13 14   10 9 8 7 6 5 4 3 2 1

ACKNOWLEDGEMENTS
The contributions of the following individuals have been gratefully received – Col Dan Barry, USAF (Ret), Art Brattkus, Col Jacksel M Broughton, USAF (Ret), Maj Murray Denton, USAF (Ret), Lt Col Allen Lamb, USAF (Ret), Capt M A Marshall, USAF (Ret), Cdr Peter Mersky, USNR (Ret), Maj Ed Rasimus, USAF (Ret), Maj Jim Rotramel, USAF (Ret), Norman Taylor and Phil Waters

FOR A CATALOGUE OF ALL BOOKS PUBLISHED BY OSPREY MILITARY AND AVIATION PLEASE CONTACT:

Osprey Direct, c/o Random House Distribution Center,
400 Hahn Road, Westminster, MD 21157
Email: uscustomerservice@ospreypublishing.com

Osprey Direct, The Book Service Ltd, Distribution Centre,
Colchester Road, Frating Green, Colchester, Essex, CO7 7DW
Email: customerservice@ospreypublishing.com

www.ospreypublishing.com

CONTENTS

FROM NUKES TO NAPES

When F-105D pilots began their first tentative combat missions over Laos in August 1964, their aircraft was still a comparatively recent USAF acquisition. Although its design dated back to September 1953, the Republic F-105's protracted development schedule meant that the 610th, and last, D-model (62-4411) was not delivered to the USAF until January 1965. The type had been preceded in frontline service by the F-105B, which had not achieved operational readiness (ORI) until January 1959, despite the prototype YF-105A having first flown on 22 October 1955.

Planning for the more capable F-105D began in mid-1957, the USAF wanting 800 examples for 11 of its Tactical Air Command (TAC) wings. However, only nine wings, and several support units, would get to fly the F-105 operationally from 1960 onwards. The following year Secretary of Defense Robert S McNamara, who had supported conventional (rather than nuclear) tactical air power, chose the multi-mission McDonnell F-4C Phantom II, cancelling additional F-105 production.

When the surviving F-105Ds returned from six years of war in Southeast Asia, having completed 20,000 combat missions and suffered 330 losses to the most concentrated air defences ever experienced, there were barely enough airframes left to equip six Air National Guard and Reserve squadrons. The F-105 had become the only US combat aircraft ever to be withdrawn from the frontline because of attrition.

Korean War experience showed that high-altitude bombers were vulnerable. Designers including Republic's Alexander Kartveli were asked to create fighter-bombers that could deliver new, small tactical nuclear weapons carried internally at Mach 1.3 from 8000+ ft. The dominant nuclear-orientated influence of Strategic Air Command

A 354th TFS F-105D takes fuel from a drogue-equipped tanker, which was a more difficult option when compared with the probe method usually employed by the Thunderchief. For correct positioning pilots tried to align the edge of the 'basket' with the metal fitting that joined the 12-ft flexible hose to the tanker's boom, but turbulence over the F-105's nose and a short, retractable, probe made this difficult. This aircraft is armed with AGM-12A Bullpups for the first Thanh Hoa bridge strike on 3 April 1965 (*USAF*)

(SAC) impelled TAC generals to seek survival for their fighter force via nuclear capability, rather than planning for 'limited conventional war' scenarios that actually faced US armed forces in the following decades.

Kartveli had a reputation for designing tough, fast fighters, notably the P-47 Thunderbolt and F-84 Thunderjet. He proposed a swept-wing F-84 derivative with a powerful Pratt & Whitney J57 turbojet engine and internal weapons bay. Under the USAF's newly instigated 'weapons system' procurement methods, Republic was awarded a contract on 25 September 1952 for 199 F-105As – Mach 1.5 fighters carrying 3500 lbs of nuclear stores internally. The end of the Korean War cut the order to just 37 aircraft – the first of many fluctuations in F-105 requirements.

In 1953 Kartveli's design used a thin wing, swept at 45 degrees and only 385 sq ft in area, giving it a high wing-loading value of 135.3 lbs per square foot (psf), with consequent limitations on manoeuvrability. By comparison, its future combat partner the F-4 Phantom II, also noted for its limited agility, had a wing loading of around 73.1 psf. It was assumed that the F-105 would not have to 'dogfight', its most likely adversary being a surface-to-air missile (SAM). The latter would be avoided by flying below its effective altitude, while hostile fighters could be escaped via superior speed. Damage-resistant hydraulic systems or protection for vulnerable areas were therefore minimised to lighten the airframe. In combat over Vietnam all of these characteristics would come into sharp focus.

Kartveli added distinctive four-piece airbrakes aft of the jet-pipe, with a ventral fin for high-speed stability. The original four T-130 machine guns were replaced by one General Electric M61A1 cannon. After long negotiations and delays, Air Staff issued General Operating Requirement (GOR) 49, which was essentially the blueprint for the F-105B with the new Pratt & Whitney J75 engine, on 1 December 1955.

Under the USAF's Cook-Craigie 'concurrency' procurement method, a new design was put straight into production on the assumption that any defects thrown up during early service use could be remedied with suitable modifications during production. Two J57-powered YF-105As and ten J75-powered YF-105Bs conducted flight-testing while production of the F-105B commenced. Fortunately, the J75 engine produced its intended 23,500 lbs of thrust in afterburner from the outset, giving production aircraft a favourable (for the time) thrust-to-weight ratio of 0.75:1, compared with 0.87:1 for the twin-engined F-4 Phantom II. The prototype's straight engine intakes caused excessive drag and were quickly

This photograph of an early *Barrel Roll* mission by a Det 2, 18th TFW flight was taken from a KC-135 tanker in January 1965. All four F-105Ds featured in the shot had become war casualties by 15 June 1967, when 61-0213 was hit during a Dong Khe attack and its pilot, Capt J W Swanson (34th TFS), was lost in the sea. 61-0192 was a 5 May 1966 operational loss with the 12th TFS, and 61-0184 was serving with the same unit on 10 August 1965 when Capt M J Kelch was forced to eject from it after flying the 37 mm flak-damaged aircraft 100 miles from the Vinh Tuy road bridge over which it had been hit. Finally, 62-4265 of the 34th TFS was lost to small arms fire on a *Barrel Roll* sortie over Laos on 10 January 1967, its pilot, Capt J P Gauley, being killed when his parachute failed to open properly after he had ejected (*USAF*)

replaced by forward-swept models with a variable position 'plug' controlled by the Bendix central air data computer to manage the airflow.

The 'area rule' concept was applied to the fuselage, giving the F-105 'coke bottle' contours and allowing it to achieve supersonic performance via decreased drag. The vertical stabiliser's area was increased by 32 per cent, with afterburner cooling intakes built in its leading edge.

Henry G Beaird made the first F-105B flight (in 54-100) on 26 May 1956. The type faced cancellation threats in 1957 when development delays caused the USAF to contemplate switching to the rival North American F-107A. Opting to stay with the F-105B (dubbed 'Thunder-chief' on 26 July 1956), the USAF duly refined its advanced equipment complement for the fighter, beginning with the AN/APN-105 Doppler navigation system and General Electric XMA-8 integrated fire-control system. Both were highly innovative to the point where the F-105 had been in service two years before they were cleared for operational use.

The Doppler system could be linked to the autopilot to return the F-105 to base without external navigation stations, and then 'hand it over' to an airfield for an instrument landing approach. In combat, as Vietnam F-105 pilot Ed Rasimus explained, 'The Doppler was a go/no go item. If your Doppler was out, your aeroplane was out. Knowing how to use it, how to update it and what its capabilities were was basic'.

The prodigious fuel consumption of the jet's J75 engine necessitated up to three drop tanks, with an optional 390-gallon tank in the bomb-bay replacing a nuclear weapon. Two 450-gallon wing tanks, angled down-wards to minimise drag, were used (freeing the bomb-bay for nuclear alert) or a 650-gallon centreline tank with external ordnance.

Three years late, the fighter finally entered service with the 335th TFS/4th TFW at Seymour Johnson AFB, North Carolina, in August 1958. The F-105's complexity required new approaches to pilot training. Lacking a two-seat variant, trainees needed 1000 hours of flying time – including 200 hours in other Century Series fighters.

Avionics were the focus of many of the early development problems, although Projects *Big Bear* and *Look Alike* (completed in November 1962) stopped fuel leaks, improved wiring and solved corrosion problems by applying water-sealing aluminised silver acrylic lacquer to the airframe. These projects usually involved grounding F-105s for extended periods, thus adding to the fighter's reputation as a maintenance nightmare. This view was not reversed until the late 1960s.

The 563rd TFS/23rd TFW deployed to Takhli RTAFB on 6 April 1965 for Operation *Two Buck Charlie*, thus becoming the first USAF unit to serve a four-month combat tour since the Korean War. By August 1965 it had amassed more combat experience than any other fighter squadron at that time. F-105D 62-4386 was lost to 85 mm AAA on a Yen Bai mission on 31 May 1966 (1Lt Leonard Ekman was rescued), but 61-0134 survived the war and finished its flying career with the Virginia ANG's 149th TFS (*USAF*)

By the end of 1962 the 4th TFW had converted to the F-105D, having resolved many of the jet's complex problems and demonstrated the qualities that were to establish it as a superb combat aircraft. These included tremendous stability throughout the speed range, with no pitch-up in high-speed manoeuvres – a problem that afflicted other early super-sonic fighters. The M61A1 was extremely accurate and the jet could deliver ordnance at low altitudes at unprecedented speeds. One of the pilots impressed by the new aircraft was Murray Denton, who recalled;

'My first impression of the F-105 was how large it was and how roomy the cockpit seemed. Coming from the F-106 Delta Dart, I couldn't believe the long take-off roll. I remember the night flights with "three bags" of fuel, and water injection for more thrust. We would use all 9000 ft of runway and milk the flaps up. It was a very stable platform, and the faster it flew the better it got. It operated well from sea level to 15,000 ft, and in military power the jet would run faster than any other aircraft at low level – it just didn't turn much! The aircraft also had a great gun and was a very stable bomber that could take hits and come home.'

However, opposition to the F-105 continued, and uncomplimentary nicknames like 'Thud' (later adopted, with ironic affection, by its pilots) alluded to its early loss rate, although it actually had the second best accident rate for a Century Series fighter. Critics also bemoaned the fighter's high cost, and the USAF proposed chopping $105,000 per jet by deleting the gun, fire suppressant in the fuel tanks, ALE-2 chaff dispenser and AN/APS-54 and AN/APS-92 radar warning systems. Fortunately for wartime pilots all but the last of these survived. Alternative savings were made on 1 April 1959 by reducing the initial F-105D order to 359 and cancelling the proposed two-seat F-105E. Only two USAFE wings (the 36th and 49th TFWs) received 203 F-105Ds between 12 May 1961 and 24 June 1963, and most of these were eventually re-deployed to Vietnam.

The first production F-105D (58-1146) made its maiden flight on 9 June 1959. It differed visually from the B-model in having a 15-inch longer nose to house the AN/ASG-19 Thunderstick fire control system and North American Autonetics R-14A radar, optimised for ground mapping. Offering a terrain avoidance mode, its limited all-weather capability came from the General Electric FC-5 flight control system.

The inclusion on these new avionics forced Republic to move the M61A1 (which occupied most of the B-model's nose) back. In an effort to save space, the weapon's dual ammunition feed chutes were replaced by a large drum. Empty shell cases and belt links had previously been returned to an ammunition box to maintain the jet's centre of gravity, but with the F-105D its ammunition was linkless, allowing spent cases to be returned to the drum. In combat, the weapon's ability to fire 100 rounds per second proved devastating for strafing AAA and transport targets.

In the cockpit, the B-model's traditional 'steam gauge' instruments were partly replaced by vertical tape displays, with pre-sets providing speed and altitude information at a glance.

The J75-P-19 had water injection from a 36-gallon tank that gave the fighter an extra 2000 lbs of thrust for 35 seconds, taking the total thrust available to 26,500 lbs at sea level. This boost was only used during take-offs, and it became a standard requirement when units were flying combat missions from Thailand. Activated by a cockpit switch, the system automatically dumped water on the runway if the pilot forgot to turn it on since the water tank was not stressed for in-flight loads.

Strengthened undercarriage units were needed to cope with the F-105D's 2000 lbs of extra take-off weight compared with the 46,998 lbs of the F-105B-20-RE. It was the world's heaviest single-engined aircraft, although pilots expected this from the Republic 'Locomotive Works'.

The F-105D's vital 'zero altitude' speed was 25 knots slower than the F-105B's 750 knots, and its stalling speed was a little higher at 181 knots.

Training for the F-105D was handled by the 4526th Combat Crew Training Squadron (CCTS) of the 4520th Combat Crew Training Wing (CCTW) at Nellis AFB, Nevada, which received its first F-105D on 1 August 1960. Classes of nine students took two-month courses in navigation and weapons systems and spent 45 hours flying the F-105, covering radar navigation and combat simulation, with an emphasis on nuclear rather than conventional weapons delivery using MN-1A bomblet dispensers on the centreline pylon or a concrete-filled replica 'nuke' in the internal bomb-bay. Little time was devoted to aerial combat – a deficiency common to most fighter training in the 1960s.

Col Jack Broughton, whose operational experience in fighters began in 1945, was among the earliest F-105 pilots to see combat;

'Most of us old heads in the "Thud" business had a good grasp on aerial combat. I don't think air-to-air was ever considered irrelevant in training, at least not at our level. We didn't have very many trainees join us during my time in Southeast Asia. We needed experienced guys to go North, and if we got a new guy we taught him all we could on-scene.'

Nellis taught experienced TAC aviators until the advent of the F-105F enabled pilots to join courses directly from advanced flight training schools. Trainees spent 120 of their 739 hours with the 4526th CCTS learning to fly the jet. A second squadron, the 4523rd CCTS, shared the training burden from October 1962 until the inactivation of both units on 20 January 1968. During 1966, as the F-105 became increasingly pivotal to the air war in Southeast Asia, the training programme passed to the 4th TFW at Seymour Johnson AFB and the 23rd TFW at McConnell AFB, Kansas, which became the F-105 Replacement Training Unit from 1 January 1966 until November 1970. The latter wing activated a new unit, the 4519th CCTS (419th TFS from 15 October 1969) on 1 August 1967 to absorb part of the Nellis training programme. Abbreviated training was introduced to counter pilot shortages in 1967, providing 60-hour courses for aviators drawn from bomber and transport units or office desk jobs. Sadly, from the first of those classes 15 of the 16 students that graduated were killed or imprisoned during the war.

A two-seat variant was approved in May 1962 as an instrument trainer for the low-altitude, all-weather nuclear mission, but the

The 334th TFS's distinctive tail markings are seen in different patterns on 61-0127 and 62-4367. An ex-36th TFW F-105D, 61-0127 was lost to AAA on 5 July 1967 with Maj Wayne Waddell of the 354th TFS at the controls – he became a PoW. 62-4367 survived missiles, MiGs and AAA until 13/14 July 1968, when Maj R K Hanna of the 333rd TFS was hit during a nocturnal strafing run but was rescued. Pilots usually refuelled 45 minutes after take-off, depending on the weapons load (*USAF*)

last 143 F-105D-31s had to be cancelled to afford 107 F-105F-1s. The second cockpit required a 31-inch fuselage extension and a vertical stabiliser that was five inches taller and 15 per cent greater in area, while the 3000-lb weight increase meant a stronger undercarriage. Fuel capacity, performance and combat capability matched the F-105D, Col Broughton being told by an experienced pilot who flew F-105Fs as single-seaters after *Rolling Thunder* that 'it was smoother, more manoeuvrable and better on fuel consumption than the D-model'.

The F-105F prototype (62-4412) flew on 11 June 1963, and deliveries began in December 1963. Although the aircraft's minimal visibility from the rear seat limited its use as a trainer, the F-model was to find other vital warfare roles. Production ended in January 1965 with F-105F 63-8366.

Having trained crews for the two USAFE wings, the 4520th CCTW generated F-105D crews for the 18th TFW, Pacific Air Forces (PACAF) in the autumn of 1962. The jets were operating from their Kadena AB, Okinawa, base via Project *Flying Fish* by the spring of 1963. The 8th TFW, based at Itazuke AB, Japan, was next to transition to the F-105D in the spring of 1963, remaining at the base until 10 July 1964.

The 8th and 18th TFWs' nuclear alert posture also required them to rotate crews and aircraft to Osan AB, South Korea. This duty of defence for Japan and Korea continued throughout the F-105's tenure in Southeast Asia, with 41st Air Division (AD) pilots spending one week per month at Osan. PACAF F-105 units performing this mission had to provide several jets to stand short-notice alert around the clock, with an internal Mk 28 or Mk 43 'special' weapon or a Mk 61 under the inboard or centreline pylon. Pilots were pre-briefed with their individually assigned targets, and they trained regularly in nuclear weapons delivery.

From 1964, pilots flying in Southeast Asia knew they risked capture by enemies who would seek to pass on their memorised knowledge of nuclear techniques and targets to Soviet or Chinese intelligence, making their imprisonment even more painful. However, in Col Broughton's opinion such thoughts were not uppermost in pilots' minds in Vietnam;

'We were like race-car drivers in that we knew it could happen to someone else, but not to us. We wanted to win the war and we did not want to get shot down. Why worry about anything else?'

These two 562nd TFS/23rd TFW F-105Ds were photographed over Laos in late 1965 armed with M117 bombs and 2.75-inch rocket pods. On 11 July 1966 61-0121 indirectly became the first F-105 to officially fall to a MiG-21 after a fight with future ace Vu Ngoc Dinh and Dong Van Song (who claimed the jet) left Maj William McClelland short of fuel. He ejected safely near the Thai border with Laos (*USAF*)

WAR IN LAOS

Following the Gulf of Tonkin incident on 2 August 1964, in which the intelligence-gathering destroyer USS *Maddox* (DD-731) was intercepted by three North Vietnamese 'Swatow' patrol boats, Fifth Air Force ordered Col Chester van Etten, CO of the 6441st TFW at Yokota AB, Japan, to deploy 18 F-105Ds to Korat Royal Thai Air Force Base (RTAFB). The 36th TFS under Lt Col Don McCance was assigned the mission, and its silver Thunderchiefs arrived at a then austere Korat on 12 August, having routed via Clark AB, in the Philippines.

Two days later the aircraft flew a rescue combat air patrol (RESCAP) mission for an 'Air America' T-28 Trojan that had been downed over the Plaine des Jarres in Laos. Called in to attack a Pathet Lao anti-aircraft artillery (AAA) site, the F-105Ds made repeated strafing runs during which Lt Dave Graben's jet (62-4371) was hit and started burning. He gained enough altitude to starve the fire of oxygen and recovered to Korat. His badly damaged aircraft got him back, but it had to be scrapped.

Graben's experience with the first combat-damaged F-105 was typical of many similar incidents during eight years of war in Southeast Asia. They illustrated the Thunderchief's toughness, despite the vulnerability of its hydraulic and fuel systems to ground fire. This mission also revealed the dangers of duelling with AAA sites.

The Gulf of Tonkin incident had prompted a quick response from Adm U S G Sharp, commander-in-chief of US Naval Forces in the region. Aircraft carriers operating with the Seventh Fleet had provided the dominant American military presence in the area from July 1964, and naval air strikes were conducted against three North Vietnamese coastal targets 72 hours after the patrol boat incident. These actions, and the arrival of 36th TFS Thunderchiefs in neutral Thailand, brought threats of intervention and increased material support for North Vietnam from China and the Soviet Union, including the promise of MiG fighters.

Gen Hunter Harris, commanding PACAF, wanted assurance that any such increase in North Vietnamese capability could be 'taken out' immediately, but President Lyndon Johnson refused substantial follow-up strikes, insisting that further action could only be in direct response to specific North Vietnamese aggression. The pattern for the war years was thereby set – hesitant responses by the US government, based on the premise that North Vietnam could be dissuaded politically from its support for Viet Cong insurgency in South Vietnam, and a preference for advice from civilians rather than frontline military experts. F-105 crews were to bear the brunt of this policy throughout the ensuing conflict.

One such blatantly aggressive act took place on 1 November 1964 when the Viet Cong infiltrated Bien Hoa AB, near Saigon, destroying ten USAF aircraft and killing four American airmen. This attack brought immediate requests from US service chiefs for B-52 strikes on Noi Bai airfield, near Hanoi, where the Vietnamese People's Air Force (VPAF) was establishing its 921st Fighter Regiment (FR) with 36 MiG-17s.

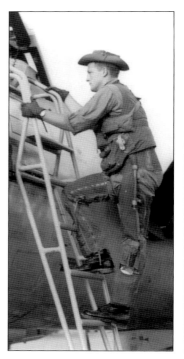

Capt Don Totten climbs aboard his F-105 in early 1965. Note the jungle knife strapped to his lower left leg, Air Commando hat (usually made by on-base tailors and covered in the pilot's mission scores) and survival kit. The latter eventually included a 0.38 Combat Masterpiece handgun, a 200-ft nylon rope to climb down from trees, six signal flares and a gold bar among roughly 80 lbs of items. Flight suits were changed after each sweaty mission (*USAF*)

The proximity of the US presidential elections resulted in Lyndon Johnson rejecting these requests – his manifesto included a resolution to avoid bombing North Vietnam. Instead, he instigated a programme of air strikes against the supply routes in the 'panhandle' area of Laos, rather than attacking the sources of those supplies in the North.

The alternatives, proposed by a State Department and Defence study group, included either intensive bombing of bridges, railways and airfields until Hanoi desisted or a 'slow squeeze' of air attacks moving from Laos into North Vietnam. This second approach allowed the use of a 'graduated response' in which the severity of the bombing would depend on North Vietnamese (and Chinese or Soviet) reactions to it. Johnson accepted a plan involving 30 days of counter-infiltration strikes in Laos, mainly by Vietnamese Air Force (VNAF) units, followed by up to six months of air strikes that advanced towards the North Vietnamese capital. The purpose of these attacks was to warn the Hanoi regime of the potential strength of American air power, hoping that this would cause the abandonment of North Vietnamese ambitions to unite Vietnam under communist rule. In fact, the attacks had quite the opposite effect, uniting the North Vietnamese behind their leaders and increasing their resolve to defend themselves at any cost. And the slow, predictable advance of the 'bombing line' enabled the VPAF to expand its defences.

It also created an extremely difficult combat environment for aircrew, who were required to perform those air strikes according to the restrictive rules of engagement (RoE) then in place. The latter prevented air power from having the decisive effect on North Vietnam that aircrew felt their skill and equipment could deliver. Combined with excessive management of the war by multiple levels of command, it led to a virtual no-win situation for those involved. In Col Jack Broughton's estimation, 'The road between wing headquarters and "higher" headquarters was a dead-end, one-way street. We could not tell them anything. They had not been there, and they demeaned those who had been there. A suggestion based on our experience of fighting the real war was an invitation to rebuke and censure. Gradualism, as directed by President Johnson and Robert McNamara, defined frustration and ensured lack of victory. Additional details and restrictions were added by the "fumble-bumble" of rank climbers and incompetent staffers who formed the various headquarters levels between the President's Tuesday "Lunch Bunch" and the warriors'.

FIRST STRIKE

F-105 missions supporting the first Laotian strike in a programme named Operation *Barrel Roll* began on 15 December 1964. The 18th TFW had supplied six 44th TFS F-105Ds to Korat several days earlier, these jets being flown by crews from the wing's 12th and 67th TFSs. The 44th had sent the first F-105Ds to Korat in April of that year for Exercise *Air Boon Choo*, testing the feasibility of operating the jet from the jungle air base.

The 44th subsequently returned to Korat in August 1964, providing fighter escort for RF-101C reconnaissance flights. Other PACAF F-105 units also performed this mission during the latter half of the year, namely the 80th, 357th and 67th TFSs. It was on one of these sorties that Capt Chuck McClarren of the 80th TFS became the first F-105 pilot to win the Distinguished Flying Cross (DFC). With Capt Neal Jones as

F-105D 62-4266, formerly with the 563rd TFS, has 50 missions marked on its nose as it awaits a top-up before continuing a late-1965 sortie to North Vietnam. From this 562nd TFS flight, only 61-0176 (later *The Jolly Roger*) survived for eventual preservation at Maxwell AFB. 61-0116 was lost to ground fire on 20 July 1966 when 355th TFW staff officer Col W H Nelson (who was killed) made a second strafing pass on a truck south of Hoa Binh. Finally, Capt John Brodak of the 354th TFS was captured near the Laotian border after ejecting from flak-damaged 62-4266, which had been hit near the Thai Nguyen target area on 14 August 1966 (*USAF*)

wingman, he was escorting Capt B L Waltz's RF-101C when it was hit by AAA near Tchepone on 21 November 1964. McClarren and Jones flew RESCAP for the downed pilot until an 'Air America' UH-34 helicopter could rescue him.

Three days earlier, 13 Korat-based F-105Ds had joined eight 613th FS F-100Ds from Da Nang, in South Vietnam, in an unsuccessful RESCAP attempt for Capt William Martin (also from the 613th TFS). His jet had been hit by AAA near Ban Senphan, in Laos, during an Operation *Yankee Team* mission – Martin had ejected, but died from injuries he had suffered when he hit rocky terrain on landing. This was a fate suffered by several F-105 pilots during the conflict in Vietnam. On 19 November a flight of Thunderchiefs destroyed the AAA site that had downed Martin's fighter.

These losses brought demands for retaliatory strikes on the supply routes in the Mu Gia Pass, but they were all rejected by the Johnson administration. Instead, Operation *Barrel Roll* began on 10 December. This limited bombing campaign included tightly regulated armed reconnaissance missions against infiltration routes in eastern central Laos. Only four strike aircraft would be allowed per mission. 80th TFS F-105Ds were detached from Korat to Da Nang for this mission in an effort to preserve Thai neutrality. The US government had instructed the Pentagon to maintain the illusion that no American air operations over North Vietnam originated from Thailand. Indeed, all personnel conducting the war in Laos were given civilian passports and sworn to secrecy. Additional restrictions included a three-day gap between missions, a 'no go' area within two miles of the South Vietnamese border and a ban on napalm.

The first *Barrel Roll* mission took place on 14 December when four F-105Ds sortied from Da Nang with what was to become the aircraft's standard ordnance load – six M117 750-lb bombs on a centreline multiple ejection rack (MER) and CBU-2A bomblet dispensers or rocket pods on the outboard pylons. Two aircraft had an alternative load of two AGM-12B Bullpup missiles on their inboard pylons and a centreline fuel tank. Two Korat-based F-105Ds escorted the RF-101C battle damage assessment (BDA) aircraft, with a CAP flight of Da Nang F-100Ds.

The 80th TFS Thunderchiefs were flying north at low altitude along Route 8 in the direction of Nape Pass when one of the pilots spotted a truck crossing a partly submerged pontoon bridge. The flight leader dropped his M117s but missed the target. The pilots pressed on with the mission, but their low speed and altitude resulted in them suffering handling problems and rapid fuel exhaustion. Airborne refuelling was not readily available at that stage of the war, so the remaining jets had to dispose of their war-loads in a safe jettison area in order to reach Da Nang.

This first mission was to be replicated on many occasions. F-105s had been designed for high-speed nuclear weapons delivery, where exact

accuracy was not required. The pilot would deliver his bomb via a 'toss' delivery manoeuvre, and he would not see his target close-up or fly in formation with other F-105s. However, on early *Barrel Roll* sorties precise visual identification of the target was needed without the assistance of the airborne forward air controllers (FAC), who greatly eased this burden later in the conflict. Visibility was often poor in the damp Laotian atmosphere, with targets frequently obscured by cloud or smoke haze from agricultural fires. Pilots struggled to haul their heavy, bomb-laden, aircraft around in tight turns at low altitudes as they attempted to keep targets in sight. At least this first mission did not encounter AAA, unlike the second 80th TFS *Barrel Roll* operation on 21 December.

On this occasion it was the F-105Ds that flew top cover for F-100Ds hitting a supply route. Heavy AAA broke up the Super Sabres' attack before they reached the target and they became disorientated. The entire force returned to Da Nang without finding another target. A few days later four more F-105s were sent on an armed reconnaissance along Route 23 and they attacked a AAA site but missed the barracks at Tchepone.

The third week of the programme brought more attacks, this time on 'suspected supply areas' (in the language of the war this often indicated no certain target), combined with similar missions by Royal Lao Air Force (RLAF) T-28s. The US government was eventually forced to concede that these early F-105 missions had caused no discernible change in North Vietnamese resolve. After this instructive early combat experience the 80th TFS returned to Yokota, but a further tour in June 1965 under Maj John P Anderson took them to Takhli RTAFB.

ESCALATION

Despite the limited results from early *Barrel Roll* activity, there was a significant increase in the pressure being applied on communist supply routes in Laos following the Viet Cong's provocative Christmas Eve attack on the Brink Hotel in Saigon, which killed two Americans. Approval was given for a bigger *Barrel Roll* mission on 13 January 1965 against the Ban Ken bridge on Route 7 in northern Laos.

Sixteen F-105Ds drawn from the 44th and 67th TFSs and led by an RF-101C 'pathfinder' aircraft were escorted by eight 401st TFW F-100D flak suppressors. Although the bridge was dropped by the F-105s' 64 M117 bombs and 16 Bullpups, the 44th TFS sustained the war's first Thunderchief loss when Capt Albert Vollmer's jet (62-4296) was downed by AAA as it made a Bullpup attack during its third pass at a AAA site. Vollmer, one of several Korean War veterans in the experienced first cadre of F-105 combat pilots, was quickly rescued. He was shot down for

Takhli's flightlines are crowded with 335th TFS (left), and 334th TFS (right) TDY F-105Ds in both silver and camouflage finishes in November 1965, shortly after the establishment of the 355th TFW at the base. 61-0156 (front right) was lost to AAA in a Thai Nguyen POL attack on 12 August 1966, Capt David Allinson ejecting near Yen Bai but being killed either on landing or during capture (*USAF*)

a second time during an armed reconnaissance on 17 August 1967, and although rescued again, his injuries precluded further combat flying.

After the Ban Ken mission many questioned the wisdom of multiple passes against defended sites and the efficacy of random armed reconnaissance missions. Adm Sharp recommended coordinated attacks to damage North Vietnamese military capability in more obvious ways. In Laos, however, moderation was still the rule thanks to the country's US Ambassador, William H Sullivan, who was a dominant influence in determining levels of American response to the insurgency. He insisted on a low-key programme of four missions a day against supply routes. However, a new operation known as *Steel Tiger* commenced in March 1965 in southern Laos adjacent to the South Vietnamese border.

At Sullivan's suggestion, flights of four F-105s and four F-4Cs were put on quick-reaction status (codenamed *Whiplash* and *Bango*, respectively) at their Thai bases to respond to requests for air strikes from the Laotian government from May 1965 until 1 November 1966. F-105s started flying *Steel Tiger* sorties on 11 April with an attack in the Ban Langkhang area, and the first rocket-armed *Whiplash* mission was flown on 23 May, controlled by a Laotian FAC aboard a C-123 *Victor Control* aircraft. At the Laotians' request, *Whiplash* missions extended from the designated *Steel Tiger* area of southern Laos into *Barrel Roll* territory in the north.

TANKERS

In-flight refuelling became vital in order to give any useful loiter time in the target area, and SAC KC-135s flew the first of their 194,687 wartime combat sorties on 9 June 1964. A pattern of colour-coded tanker 'tracks' was soon established, covering routes to the targets, but not so obviously that the defences could guess those targets. Refuelling altitudes were set between 7000 ft and 19,000 ft, although a fully loaded F-105 became hard to handle on the tanker above 18,500 ft. For refuelling over Laos, the tankers met their 'customers' via TACAN Channel 97. Sometimes, they would press northwards beyond their designated limits to meet fighters that were nearing fuel starvation. As Col Jack Broughton remembered;

'The tanker guys always did their best to support us. I have very personal knowledge of one crew who absolutely saved my wingman and myself from having to bail out over Laotian cannibal country. We put them up for a medal. SAC killed the medal and disciplined them for crossing an imaginary line, and for giving us "get home" fuel to save us.'

For F-105 pilots, target identification remained a problem. Unreliable map coordinates provided insufficient guidance in identifying Pathet Lao-occupied buildings, semi-hidden in featureless jungle. Target intelligence from local observers was sketchy too, and the enemy moved fast. Many mission briefings specified bridges as the primary target, but often these were planks across a stream or pontoons used only at night. Hitting them

These 357th TFS jets, photographed on 11 November 1965, are armed with Mk 82 Snakeye bombs. As Ed Rasimus explained, 'You got better at the mission by using every bit of information you could absorb. The end result was "situational awareness" – the four-dimensional picture in your head of the combat arena. You knew where you were, where you were going to be, what the time-sequence was and as much about the defensive reaction as you could absorb both in pre-planning and through real-time data. Getting the most out of your RHAW gear, knowing what your ECM pods were doing and when, integrating the radio calls and prioritising which were important, all led to survival. Learning how to manage the various inputs so that you could deal with the data was part of becoming a fighter pilot. It got tougher as your responsibilities grew with the addition of a wingman, then a flight of four and ultimately perhaps the whole strike package' (*USAF*)

with an F-105 was hard enough, but having to re-attack them repeatedly was demoralising. Since the US government would not deploy the vast numbers of troops needed to control the area, USAF pilots were given the task, sometimes assisted by *Shining Brass* observation squads who provided FAC guidance. A successful attack using this technique took place on 18 October 1965 when 38 F-105s and F-4Cs were called in to destroy six large enemy supply and ammunition bunkers.

'The biter, bit'. Groundcrew point out AAA damage to the gun port and radome of an F-105D (possibly 62-4361), which still managed to complete its mission. Flak-damaged Thunderchiefs returned their pilots to base on numerous occasions (*USAF*)

Three months earlier, Gen William Westmoreland (commander of US forces in South Vietnam) had requested O-1E Bird Dogs to provide better FAC guidance, but the Laotians insisted that they should be flown by RLAF pilots, who would then be debriefed by Americans. Mistakes occurred, however, resulting in extensive financial compensation and political 'repair work' with Laotian authorities. For example, on 30 September 1965 four F-105Ds mistook fishermen's traps for a pontoon bridge, strafed them and hit two villagers. Pilots, rather than the RoE, were usually blamed for 'mis-strikes'.

Night missions were also flown in an attempt to catch the 300+ trucks moving down the supply routes defended by 300+ AAA batteries and maintained by around 25,000 labourers. However, the difficulty in detecting these vehicles, usually hidden under jungle top-cover, increased pressure from the Joint Chiefs of Staff (JCS) to begin action against the source of the supplies, rather than waiting until they were en route to the insurgents. Trucks were well camouflaged, and they hid under cover in small groups along roads equipped with food and rest and repair areas. Damaged vehicles were sometimes left visible to lure pilots into flak traps, and fires were started on the roadside as fake 'burning targets'. For much of the war pilots were forbidden to bomb more than 200 yards from the edge of a road, allowing trucks fairly safe refuge beyond that point.

As road traffic increased extra missions were flown, particularly against vulnerable 'choke' points in the Mu Gia and Nape passes, where blockages by damaged trucks or bomb craters would temporarily delay traffic. On 16-17 July 1965 F-105s dropped 18,000 lbs of ordnance on these choke points, including delay-fused bombs to disrupt repairs.

There were some major successes. A *Tally Ho* strike across the border in Route Package (RP) I in July 1966 uncovered a 100-ton ammunition dump some 200 ft long and 10 ft high. Hidden under foliage, it was revealed when bomb blasts from an attack on three trucks blew away the cover, giving F-105 pilots the 'secondary explosions' they hoped to see. Generally though, the *Steel Tiger* truck score remained low. From July to September 1966 only 73 vehicles could be reasonably claimed as destroyed or damaged. It was calculated that six F-105 sorties were needed to destroy each truck, rather than one mission to destroy a shipload of brand new vehicles still on the docks at Haiphong.

In December 1965, under a programme called *Tiger Hound*, USAF FACs started flying the O-1Es assigned to Det 1 of the 505th Tactical Control Group at Nakhon Phanom RTAFB. An RLAF observer occupied the back seat, although many spoke poor English. F-105Ds flew the first *Tiger Hound* mission on 5 December – one of 809 tactical sorties made by US aircraft against the 'trails' network that month.

When F-105s could find their targets considerable damage was caused. Whole convoys could be wiped out by destroying the first and last vehicles with gunfire or 2.75-inch rockets and then bombing the rest. However, it became clear that the volume of traffic was increasing much faster than the available air power could handle. FAC pilots were range-limited to 200 miles from their Nakhon Phanom base, and information from ground 'spies' often took more than 12 hours to pass through the Laotian government's administrative network. It then required photo-reconnaissance evidence to support a strike, followed by up to a week to get target clearance. By the time the F-105 bases were able to 'frag' missions the convoy or troop concentration had often moved elsewhere.

To extend the F-105s' attacks into the night a programme called *Gate Guard* began on 1 May 1966 in which jets flew with *Blindbat* C-130s (or occasionally RB-66Bs), which illuminated targets with flares. Bombing under these conditions brought the dual threats of pilot vertigo and unseen AAA against well-illuminated F-105s. These night missions soon passed to the Ubon-based F-4Cs of the 497th TFS 'Night Owls' and the A-26Ks of the 609th Special Operations Squadron at Nakhon Phanom.

The commencement of B-52 *Arc Light* attacks in December 1965 caused targeting safety issues, and created an extra task for F-105 pilots, who had to overfly the bombers' route, reporting on any SA-2 threats.

The arrival of the B-52s in the skies over Laos also created a logistical problem for the Thunderchief units. The bomber's enormous payloads (48 M117s) rapidly exhausted PACAF stores, reducing the sortie levels for all aircraft in the war zone by up to 15 per cent. Suitable bombs were shipped in from US bases worldwide. Robert McNamara denied the shortage, blaming it on poor distribution of stocks. Even so, F-105s were often seen heading for targets with partial bomb-loads due to shortages of M117 or CBU-2 weapons and fuses. Sortie rates had to be maintained, and there was competition between the USAF and US Navy over this.

Re-painted areas on the fin of 59-1729 show various changes in serial and code presentation during its time at Takhli – a base area noted for its king cobras, extremes of climate and lack of local amenities. This aircraft, christened *Takhli Taxi* and *Andy Capp* at different times, remained in service with the 457th TFS AFRES at Tinker AFB until July 1978. Its outboard pylons support LAU-3 pods made from treated paper, with a metal outer skin and frangible paper nose-caps. Their contents, 19 2.75-inch FFAR rockets with various types of warhead, brought the total weight to about 500 lbs per pod. The jet's forward two M117 bombs have been fitted with fuse extenders to cause wide blast destruction at SAM and AAA sites. Fuse extenders could only be attached to the upper, forward pair of bombs due to weapon clearance issues on the centreline MER (*USAF*)

From March 1966 Thai bases were permitted to load napalm on their F-105s following a request to Laotian Prime Minister Souvanna Phouma. The Laotian army often benefited from USAF strikes, not least in July 1966 when 38 F-105s prevented the North Vietnamese Army (NVA) from taking Thakhek, on the Mekong River, and dividing Laos in two. The jets dropped 150,000 lbs of bombs, causing heavy NVA casualties.

Although the Seventh Air Force had hoped to shift more of the air strike responsibility to the RLAF or USAF A-1Es, by mid-1966 more than 90 per cent of the bombing in central Laos had been undertaken by F-105s and 'Night Owl' F-4s, which continued to average 18 sorties daily into the autumn. Throughout 1967 the veteran A-1Es, supported by USAF A-26Ks and RLAF T-28s, actually demolished three times as many trucks (996 claimed) as the F-105/F-4 team at a tenth of the operating cost. However, the piston-engined types were becoming vulnerable to the increased levels of flak in Laos, and losses were considered unsustainable.

For this reason alone Gen Westmoreland preferred jets because he thought that they could evade the increasingly heavy AAA placed on the trails network, although later statistics showed that 20 F-105s and 13 F-4s were lost over Laos up to February 1968, compared with 28 A-1s.

Although the risk of being hit by AAA in Laos was not as great as when flying over North Vietnam, the chances of being rescued after ejecting over the jungle were much the same. A pilot's survival relied heavily on cooperation from other fighters, the rescue services and 'Lady Luck', as Col Jack Broughton explained;

'We all knew that if we had to punch out over the North or over Laos we would be at the mercy of brutal people, and that we could expect inhumane torture at best. Fear of capture was the worst fear we knew.'

Hal Bingaman, Col Broughton's 'favourite deputy strike leader' added;

'When I accepted "A" Flight command of the 354th TFS in September 1966 my forerunner told me of being ordered to Clark Field, in the Philippines, to identify a recovered body of one of his pilots who had bailed out over the Plain of Jars, in Laos. He had been found hanging from a tree, still in his parachute, stripped naked and flayed of his skin.'

When the 469th TFS's 1Lt Dick Hackford was hit by AAA on yet another truck park attack in the Ban Karai area of Laos on 22 May 1966, 1Lt Ed Rasimus in the 421st TFS's 'Pine' flight saw his blazing F-105D (58-1164) dive into the jungle, leaving only a trace of smoke to mark where it had crashed. Luckily, Rasimus saw Hackford's parachute and called in the rescue crews from Ubon and Nakhon Phanom. 'Buick' flight of F-4Cs from Ubon provided cover, but could not communicate directly by radio with the departing F-105s. The 'Buick' crews searched for Dick Hackford but could not locate him before they too had to leave with 'bingo' fuel. Fortunately, an A-1 'Sandy' pilot was able to supervise the rescue and Hackford was soon aboard an HH-3E helicopter.

Not all rescue attempts ended in success, however. Maj Alonzo Johnson, flying F-105D 62-4396 with the 333rd TFS on 27 October 1966, was also hit by AAA and crashed in flames. A parachute was sighted, a rescue beeper sounded and the recovery effort was mounted, but he was never found. Missions that required strafing runs in the deep, high-sided karst valleys of the region were also hazardous, as there was little room to 'jink' and evade flak.

Laden down with survival gear and a backpack parachute, Col Jack Broughton, Vice Wing Commander of the 355th TFW, climbs into his F-105D 62-4338 *Alice's Joy* (*Col Jack Broughton*)

In an attempt to improve sortie rates and accuracy during the monsoon season, when poor visibility often prevented strikes for weeks (the 1966 monsoon saw more than 1500 F-105 sorties cancelled), several innovations were introduced. MSQ-77 *Combat Skyspot* used ground radar stations that had been established during the summer of 1966 at four sites in South Vietnam and at Nakhon Phanom, in Thailand. The radar 'skin-painted' a flight of strike aircraft at distances of up to 50 miles, or 190 miles if the jets carried an SST-181 X-band radar beacon. The system needed clear line-of-sight, however, and could only control one strike flight at a time against a single target, with five-minute gaps between flights.

F-105D 61-0134 *SWEET CAROLINE* of the 357th TFS prepares to take on fuel during a 1969 mission to Laos. The aircraft is armed with Mk 82 and Mk 84 ordnance. Tanking could be hazardous even in fair weather in broad daylight. Two 333rd TFS F-105Ds collided on 3 August 1967 when one pilot unexpectedly banked away to the right rather than left after refuelling and was hit by another jet moving towards the boom. Only one pilot escaped from the resultant fireball. *SWEET CAROLINE* survived the war to operate with the Virginia ANG from 1971 to 1976 (*via Norm Taylor*)

A *Skyspot* operator transmitted a signal to a pocket-sized transponder in the lead strike aircraft, giving it a precise command to drop ordnance. The F-105s flew in formation, straight and level, at 20,000 ft, usually above a cloud base, and dropped together. The first *Skyspot* strike was in RP I in June 1966, where the AAA was of a smaller calibre than in RP VI, but equally threatening, and over Laos on 6 July. Some 10,000+ *Skyspot* sorties had been flown by the end of 1966, replacing pathfinder-led strikes in poor weather. In South Vietnam, mixed strike formations were flown with US Navy and US Marine Corps aircraft. Whenever BDA could establish accurate results it showed that the average circular area of probability was 300 ft, which was sufficiently accurate to allow this method of delivery to remain in use both in Laos and North Vietnam.

F-105s continued to fly missions into Laos because the USAF was officially prevented from attacking enemy logistics closer to their source in North Vietnam. Indeed, for much of the war no attacks were permitted on the key supply areas around Hanoi and Haiphong, so hitting the route trails was the only option available. Laotian operations were a vital part of the F-105's contribution to the war, but by 1966 USAF commanders felt that these aircraft would be better employed on Operation *Rolling Thunder*, which had seen attacks commence against targets in North Vietnam in March of the previous year.

F-105D 62-4230 from the 354th TFS cruises over dense Laotian forest in November 1969. Identifying targets or downed pilots in terrain such as this presented enormous difficulties for American aviators (*USAF via Chris Hobson*)

ROLLING THUNDER

The *Rolling Thunder* campaign was the product of many compromises and numerous authoritative, rival voices seeking to control the conduct of the war. Foremost was President Johnson, who still hoped for a negotiated peace, and sought to restrain his JCS, many of whom wanted quick, decisive action against Hanoi. In South Vietnam the dominant influence was Gen Westmoreland's Military Assistance Command, Vietnam (MACV), based in Saigon, which supported Johnson's doctrine of 'graduated response'. Staffed in the main by US Army officers, it tended to regard air power essentially as support for the ground troops, and it had McNamara's ear in most matters.

A second tier of command below MACV involved PACAF's Thirteenth Air Force, the 2nd AD (redesignated the Seventh Air Force from 1 April 1966), the Air Operations Centre at Udorn RTAFB and the various strands of US Navy command in Southeast Asia. For USAF operations this chain of command often presented a Gordian knot of conflicting orders, multiple levels of decision making and delay that was to hamstring much of its initiative in the war against North Vietnam.

At the spear-tip of that endeavour throughout the campaign were the F-105 crews at RTAFBs Korat and Takhli, although their operations over North Vietnam from these airfields remained officially secret until 9 March 1967. Their achievement in reaching and hitting their targets through unprecedented levels of defences, restrictive RoE and increasing domestic political opposition remains unique in military history.

In February 1965 the Pentagon was instructed to send four extra TAC squadrons to South Vietnam and Thailand in response to escalating Viet Cong attacks. Increasing demands for F-105 sorties ended the temporary duty (TDY) assignments that TAC units had been making to Southeast Asia. Four-month TDYs were expensive and rotated crews just as they were gaining experience and proficiency. In Operation *Ready Alpha*, the 355th TFW was assigned a permanent change of station (PCS) to Takhli from George AFB, California, where it had first accepted F-105Ds in September 1962. Col Jack Broughton was involved in this process;

'In June 1965, after graduating from the National War College, I was assigned to the 6441st AD at Yokota AB as Deputy Director of Operations. We were involved with building Takhli RTAFB, supplying and coordinating TDY pilots and ground personnel and supporting the transition of the 355th TFW into an operational configuration at Takhli. I moved to full-time duty as Vice Wing Commander in June 1966.'

The wing also acquired the 41st Tactical Reconnaissance Squadron (TRS), which took on Det 1 of the 25th Tactical Reconnaissance Wing (TRW) equipped with B-66B Destroyers. These jets were later modified into EB/RB-66B electronic warfare/pathfinder aircraft and performed roles that would be crucial to F-105 operations.

At Korat, 155 miles east of Takhli, the 388th TFW reactivated on 14 March 1966 as 'parent' unit for the 421st, 469th and, later, the 13th and

62-4356 *MUMBLES* of the 34th TFS leads an 'elephant walk' of Korat F-105s along the taxiway after visiting the arming area for panel and tyre checks and 'pulling the pins' to arm all ordnance. KC-135 tankers usually took off 20 minutes ahead of the F-105s (*USAF*)

The 34th TFS's *MUMBLES*, flanked by 60-0449 007 and 61-0194 *The Avenger*, are poised for take-off from Korat's runway. Each jet has 13,500 lbs of bombs to deliver. The aircraft usually left the runway at around 195 knots, with gear raised at 220 knots. A lenticular shock-wave pattern in the exhaust showed that the afterburner was operating well (*USAF*)

34th TFSs. Having converted to the F-105D in October 1962, the 388th was replaced at McConnell AFB by the 23rd TFW in February 1964.

Prior to the advent of PCS wings, Thai-based units were controlled in the early stages of *Rolling Thunder* by two provisional wings. The 6234th TFW was at Korat from 5 April 1965, while at Takhli, the 6441st TFW (Provisional) was established in May 1965 and replaced by the 6235th TFW on 1 July. It controlled the F-105 units until the 355th TFW took over on 8 November. The wing also had an EB/RB-66B det, initially from the 9th TRS, and after 20 October 1965 from the 41st TRS.

Following the US Navy/VNAF *Flaming Dart* strikes in February 1965, the US government approved *Rolling Thunder* the following month as a series of tightly controlled strikes, avoiding civilian casualties as it progressing northwards from the Demilitarised Zone (DMZ). President Johnson and his advisors rejected JCS demands for focused attacks on key industrial, logistical and transport centres in Hanoi and Haiphong, as well as MiG bases, fearing that the USSR and China would intervene.

In April 1964, the JCS had listed 94 suggested targets, including the crucial Paul Doumer and Thanh Hoa bridges, *before* the Gulf of Tonkin incident. History has proven President Johnson's military leaders right in dismissing the Sino-Soviet threat, but plans were in place to import a huge US force had such intervention occurred. A further, crippling, restriction on *Rolling Thunder* was the US government's (particularly Secretary of Defense McNamara's) belief that air power could never win the war, but only persuade Hanoi to negotiate. In mid-1965 McNamara summed up the Johnson administration's view on the subject when he stated, 'We don't believe that bombing in the North will drive the North Vietnamese to the bargaining table or force them to cease their terror tactics and subversion.'

Rolling Thunder, originally planned to last a few weeks, and always to be seen, according to McNamara, as 'subordinate to the air-to-ground operations in South Vietnam', was therefore interrupted by a series of negotiating 'bombing pauses'. The campaign eventually ended in March 1968 when President Johnson, who had wanted a quick end to the war that had been forced upon him, admitted publicly that it had failed, and that he would not be seeking Presidential re-election later that year.

The offensive started hesitantly when its first four missions were delayed by an attempted coup in Saigon and then cancelled by bad weather. Finally, on 2 March 1965, *Rolling Thunder* 'Program 5' hit two target areas – the Xom Bong ammunition depot and barracks just above the DMZ and Quang Khe, North Vietnam's southernmost naval base. Xom Bong was attacked by 25 F-105Ds, with 16 more supporting the strikers, as were 20 B-57s, eight flak-suppression F-100s and a four-ship F-100 MiGCAP. Twenty more F-105s, along with 25 F-100s and a squadron of VNAF A-1Hs, hit Quang Khe. Five aircraft did not return, including three F-105Ds from the 67th TFS.

The F-105s from the 12th and 67th TFSs had successfully destroyed their AAA targets, saving the strike flights from suffering any losses, but at a cost of three jets. All the downed pilots from the unit were rescued, including Capt Robert Baird, who ejected just seconds before his F-105D (61-0214) hit the ground. The two other Thunderchiefs that were lost gave an early demonstration of their toughness by getting their pilots (Capt K Spagnola, in F-105D 62-4325, and Maj George Panas in F-105D 62-4260) over friendly territory before they had to bail out.

The US government's 'Vietnamization' policy required VNAF units to participate in early *Rolling Thunder* strikes, but their poor readiness delayed the second 'program' until 14 March, when Gen Nguyen-cao-Ky, commander of the VNAF, led a raid with F-105 and F-100 flak suppressors and a MiGCAP against Tiger Island, off the coast of North Vietnam. The next day 20 F-105Ds participated in an attack by 137 aircraft on Phu Qui ammunition depot, south of Hanoi. As well as their M117 and 2.75-inch rocket armament, the jets carried napalm canisters – the first authorised use of this weapon. Napalm was effective against supply dumps and barracks, while bombs were preferred for hardened structures and rockets or CBU-2s for AAA sites and water-borne targets.

Despite worldwide condemnation, the encouraging results of these early attacks prompted USAF Chief-of-Staff Gen John Paul McConnell to seize the initiative from MACV and propose a 28-day campaign to force the North Vietnamese, who had actually been expecting a massive onslaught, to back down. This was extended into a four-phase proposal by the JCS, concentrating first on the transport network in southern North Vietnam, then on the vital railway lines to China, followed by the mining of the main ports and bombing of war stocks in Hanoi and Haiphong. Finally, any other valuable targets (excluding airfields) would be neutralised. Adm Sharp, whose carrier aircraft had better *Iron Hand* anti-radar weapons than the USAF at that time, also advocated a day of attacks to wreck North Vietnam's radar warning network. McNamara agreed to the targeting of three sites only.

On the first *Rolling Thunder* mission without a VNAF component on 22 March, eight 67th TFS F-105s led by unit CO Lt Col Robinson

Risner attacked the 'Moon Cone' radar site at Vinh Son. Based at Okinawa since 1963, Risner had flown a mission every day since arriving on a TDY at Korat, his jet frequently taking hits. Over Vinh Son, Risner's F-105D (62-4233) was struck again by AAA, and this time he ejected offshore and was picked up by an HU-16B amphibian. The rescued pilot's photograph appeared on the cover of *Time* magazine, which was unfortunately noticed by his interrogators in Hanoi when Risner was shot down for a second time on 16 September.

Two more F-105 anti-radar attacks were made in March. While *Iron Hand* strikes disrupted the enemy's expanding early-warning radar network, targets were chosen on the basis that they 'should continue to avoid the effective ground-control interception range of VPAF MiGs'. In an effort to provide the strike aircraft with further protection, McNamara allowed a contingent of 45th TFS F-4C Phantom IIs to deploy to Ubon RTAFB on 4 April, and they were available to provide MiGCAP for F-105 strikes, replacing F-100 and F-104 fighters from 7 April. The unit scored its first MiG kills during a 10 July 1965 F-105 strike near Yen Bai.

BRIDGE STRIKES

The second phase of *Rolling Thunder* began in April 1965, and it saw US air power concentrating on the North's numerous road and railway bridges. For F-105 pilots, this was to become one of the most demanding and costly chapters of the entire war. Initially, the attacks, like those in Phase 1, remained below the 20th parallel, but from *Rolling Thunder 9* they crept further north. Three bridges were targeted by Adm Sharp, with the 'Ham Rong' ('Dragon's Jaw') bridge at Thanh Hoa – only 70 miles south of Hanoi – being allocated to the USAF. Carrying vital road and rail traffic south from Hanoi across the Son Ma River, the bridge was well defended by AAA, which would exact a heavy toll on F-105 units through to 1972. Constructed with Chinese guidance in 1964, the 56 ft-wide Thanh Hoa bridge spanned 540 ft. Massively over-built in steel and concrete, it was far stronger than mission planners had anticipated.

The first maximum effort strike on the bridge on 3 April was performed by 46 F-105s with 254 M117s, 32 AGM-12A Bullpups and 266 2.75-inch rockets. Lt Col Risner and the 67th TFS from Korat led the raid, with support from Takhli's 354th TFS. The Bullpups proved ineffective despite accurate hits on key structural points and the bombs caused only superficial damage. F-105Ds were equipped with a small control stick for the pilot to steer the Bullpup after firing it in a 20-degree dive at the target from 18,000 ft. This required considerable coordination and the pilot's full attention (when he would rather have been looking out for SAMs or AAA). A separate pass was required for each launch.

Risner took yet another hit during the attack but returned safely to base, where he planned the next day's follow-up strike as requested by Gen McConnell. This time Bullpups were replaced by M117s on all 48 F-105s assigned to the mission. There were no flak suppressors either, as one of the seven 401st TFW F-100 pilots performing that hazardous task had been killed the previous day. Risner's plan was marred by poor visibility over the target and delays with the tankers which meant that several flights had to orbit ten miles south of the bridge to await their bombing times. 'Zinc' flight of the 354th TFS, away from MiGCAP

Spotless F-105D 58-1157 of the 388th TFW was photographed shortly after having depot-level maintenance completed. Upon returning from a mission to their Thai bases, the jets' crew chiefs would check the pilots' comments on the Form 781 for any mechanical problems that had arisen during the mission. They would also check engine oil levels and refill the 'booster' water-tank from an ML-1 de-mineralised water cart, after which they would attach a tow-bar to the nose-wheel and push the 'Thud' back into its revetment. The jet was then attached to earth wires and single-point refuelled with JP-4. A re-packed drag-chute would then be inserted, with difficulty, into its compartment by a technician who jumped onto the 'chute bay door, while hanging onto the rudder, to shut and latch it. After checking the engine for FOD, the armament crew were called in to hang bombs while 'gun plumbers' refilled and checked the cannon. Finally, with a protective mask in place, the crew chief replenished the liquid oxygen from a green-painted cart and re-filled the pilot's ice-water bottles just before the next mission (*USAF*)

protection, was jumped by four 921st FR MiG-17s (flying from Noi Bai) from high altitude as it orbited at 375 knots laden with bombs and unable to avoid the VPAF fighters.

MiG flight leader Tran Hanh closed on Maj Frank Bennett's F-105D (59-1754), firing his three heavy cannon to deadly effect. Bennett headed out to sea and ejected from his badly damaged aircraft, although he drowned near the island of Hon Me before rescue could be attempted. As the F-105Ds had turned to try and face their attackers, Tran Hanh's wingman, Le Minh Huan, fired at the Thunderchief (59-1764) flown by Capt James Magnusson, who also died when his jet crashed in flames. Le Minh Huan was then shot down, almost certainly by Capt Don Kilgus of the 416th TFS in the F-100D's only (unconfirmed) wartime kill. Two other MiGs were also lost, seemingly to their own inaccurate AAA. President Johnson saw the MiG kill as politically inflammatory, stating that he 'did not want any more MiGs shot down' (one possible reason why Kilgus' claim was never confirmed). A third F-105D (62-4217 of the 67th TFS 'Steel' flight) was hit by AAA over the target and Capt 'Smitty' Harris captured.

Despite having suffered more than 300 hits, the 40-ft thick concrete of the 'Dragon's Jaw' still stood, and the bridge remained useable until 1972. The two 354th TFS F-105Ds downed by the 921st FR were the first US aircraft lost in aerial combat during the war. The MiG threat was countered partly by the provision of five EC-121D *Big Eye* radar picket aircraft at Tan Son Nhut from 4 April to cooperate with 45th TFS F-4Cs.

The 354th flew 1132 sorties and sustained five more losses before the end of its TDY on 12 June 1965. Four pilots were rescued, while the fifth, 1Lt Robert Peel (whose father had been a pilot with the Royal Flying Corps in World War 1), was imprisoned after being hit by AAA on 31 May during one of the many repeat attacks on the 'Dragon's Jaw'. He was flying 62-4381 *'Give 'em 'L'* at the time – relatively inconspicuous nicknames had begun to appear on many F-105s at this time, and they were usually tolerated at wing level as a welcome morale booster.

After the first encounters with the Thanh Hoa Bridge, the 354th TFS returned to transport hunting, taking part in a 16-aircraft F-105 attack on railway lines and Route 9 on 5 April in which two locomotives and a truck convoy were hit. Capt T Gay's F-105D 59-1742 was lost to AAA, the pilot being rescued by a USAF HH-43 Huskie helicopter.

Rolling Thunder 10, between 9 and 15 April, targeted five more bridges and two radar sites. Thunderchief units destroyed highway bridges at Khe Kienm, Qui Vinh and Phuong Can, and five more were struck in *Rolling Thunder 11*. The Dien Chau and Thai Hai bridges were partially dropped with 296 M117 bombs on 16 April, when F-105s mounted the biggest one-day onslaught on North Vietnam's bridges to date. Amongst the units committed to this operation was the 36th TFS of the 41st AD, which had returned on 6 March for its second combat tour, this time as a PCS squadron. Its arrival at Takhli RTAFB 'opened' the base for F-105

Crew access was via a 12-ft ladder that usually wore paint off the fuselage where it rested ahead of the intake. Access to the aircraft's underside was much more comfortable for F-105 groundcrew than for personnel assigned to the F-4 Phantom II, although ladders and platforms were needed for most tasks. This BLU-1C/B (napalm) armed F-105D is receiving attention to its nose landing–gear (*USAF*)

operations, as it had done at Korat in August of the previous year. With part of the 561st and the 563rd TFSs at Takhli, the 36th TFS continued to pound bridge targets in the south of North Vietnam, barracks at Hon Gio, Phu Van and Vu Con and, inevitably, the Thanh Hoa bridge – North Vietnam's most heavily defended target.

F-105 units flew a particularly heavy attack on the Mu Gia Pass staging area on 17 April that saw the USAF sustain its first casualty in this target area. Capt Sam Woodworth, possibly suffering from target fixation, failed to pull out of his dive-attack. Both he and his F-105D (61-0171) were from the 563rd TFS, which was one of two 23rd TFW units on a TDY from McConnell AFB to Takhli that commenced on 6 April as part of Operation *Two Buck Charlie*. Despite this early loss, the 563rd destroyed six highway bridges during April, and also participated in Operation *Fact Sheet*, which saw four million propaganda leaflets dropped over the North.

April had ended with attacks on eight more bridges and seven ferry crossings in *Rolling Thunder 12*, and the F-105 wings destroyed these within a week. They were also allowed to plan their bombing runs as 'successive waves' rather than a single, closely spaced attack, and restrictions on armed reconnaissance missions were reduced to allow targets of opportunity to be found. Although five F-105s took damage from AAA on these missions, there were no further losses that month.

The next two 'programs', *Rolling Thunder 13/14*, in May focused another 42 missions on transportation targets, and including a strike on the Thanh Hoa bridge on the 7th. Twenty-eight F-105s were central to a 64-aircraft package led by Maj Charles Watry of the 354th TFS, dropping 356 M117s and firing 304 2.75-inch rockets at the mighty structure and its increased defences. Watry was awarded a Silver Star for remaining in the target area to direct the strike despite his aircraft's serious fuel leakage following a AAA hit. The only loss was F-105D 59-1718, its pilot, Maj R E Lambert, returning home in an HU-16B after bailing out into the sea. The bridge was damaged once again, but useable even after two further strikes later that same day. Tactics were revised as a result.

M117s lacked penetration for the task, particularly when they were fused wrongly. Further attacks were delayed until the AGM-12C Bullpup became available. Also, large formations of F-105s over the target simultaneously did not help pilots to concentrate on aim points, so smaller formations of one or two flights were used instead. Much better results were achieved the following day when 28 F-105s demolished the barracks at Xom Trung Hoa.

On 10 May President Johnson declared a five-day bombing pause which failed to speed up peace negotiations but involved the F-105 force in 175 'visual reconnaissance' missions and more leaflet-dropping – F-105 squadrons did most of the leaflet drops in 1965.

A persistent problem in the heat of battle was radio discipline. The airwaves were often overloaded with warnings, both within the strike force and from powerful external airborne and land-based transmitting agencies, sometimes interrupting what pilots actually needed to hear. If an aviator ejected, his rescue beeper would blot out the radio frequency with a shrill wail. Signals from radar-homing and warning (RHAW) equipment would also fill a pilot's headset, as could the 'hot mike' between cockpits in the two-seat F-105F. Col Jack Broughton recalled;

'We did brief that pilots were to speak on the radio only when necessary. Often, in tense times, flight leaders would have to tell individuals to shut up, but excited chatter was often a fact of combat life. When you packed lots of fast-moving machinery into a small ballpark, with good buddies getting blown up or punching out, it was difficult not to become a bit emotional. The worthless SAM and MiG calls from our four-engined radar observers flying out over the water were a pain. They usually came at the wrong time, and they blocked all other transmissions.'

When the more complex Project *Wild Weasel* F-105F/Gs were introduced the communications overload increased further. Pilot Dan Barry remembered, 'I think that we would all reach task saturation at times just dealing with the audio from the UHF, Guard channel, intercom, the tones from the various onboard systems and the missile seeker heads. The F-105 was a pretty antiquated jet by the late 1960s, and any improvements in automation would have been appreciated.'

LOSSES

In May the target list expanded to include several ammunition storage areas, and the 563rd TFS suffered three more losses during the course of the month. On the 9th Capt Robert Wistrand (in F-105D 62-4408) was hit by ground fire while attacking a AAA battery in Laos' Mu Gia Pass. He did not eject. Six days later, in a tragic operational accident, Capt Robert Greskowiak perished when his heavily-loaded F-105D (62-4374) lost power on take-off and crashed off the end of Takhli's runway, killing five civilians and wrecking a Buddhist temple. Finally, on 18 May Capt David Hrdlicka (in F-105D 59-1753) was also downed over Laos during one of the squadron's ongoing *Steel Tiger* missions. Although he ejected and was captured, Hrdlicka subsequently died in captivity some three years later.

From 22 May better weather permitted the first attack on a target above the 20th parallel when 40 F-105s seriously damaged barracks at Quang Soui, 60 miles from Hanoi, and the Phu Qui ammunition depot. The Thunderchiefs also flew joint missions with VNAF Skyraiders against barracks at Phu Le and Vu San. As these strikes proved, the 'thunder' was steadily rolling northwards in response to

Loading an F-105's 'standard' centreline complement of six M117s was facilitated by an MJ-1 'jammer' weapons loader, but plenty of muscle was still needed to accurately position the bombs too (*USAF*)

Hanoi's intransigence, although the bitter truth was that bridges and highways were being repaired within five to thirty days of US attacks, and 'barracks' were often wooden structures that could be replaced quickly too. Rather than negotiating, Hanoi just increased its army of labourers.

Only 22 of the JCS list of 95 targets had been hit by June 1965, and few had suffered long-term damage, yet Gen Westmoreland persuaded the US government to concentrate its efforts on South Vietnam. Nevertheless, F-105s, with some F-4 support, were responsible for 55 per cent of the bombing of the North at this point in the war, and they were coming increasingly under threat from the enlarged MiG force that the JCS became more determined to remove through the bombing of its airfields. Once again, McNamara refused all such requests, and inevitably Noi Bai's MiG-17s challenged the Thunderchief flights again.

The first encounter in which F-105s fired at MiG-17s came on 24 June when two VPAF jets intercepted the 'high' element of a flight of Thunderchiefs whose pilots fortunately saw them at their 'six o'clock' position. Flying 5000 ft lower, the second element climbed to meet them, and one MiG broke away to escape. The 'high' element pursued the second MiG and fired at it, but the jet turned hard and escaped.

Rolling Thunder continued unabated through the summer, with a two-weekly cycle of attacks shared equally with the US Navy. Big F-105 strikes were launched during this period against the Yen Bai and Yen Son ordnance depots, the latter covering 60 acres and yielding vast secondary explosions. The 563rd TFS amply demonstrated the Thunderchief's maximum bomb-load when six aircraft were deployed to Tan Son Nhut on 25 June, each dropping 16 M117s on Viet Cong positions en route.

New weapons were also added to the F-105's arsenal at this time too. On 11 July, jets from the 12th TFS laid MLU-10 delayed-action mines along a main rail route to Hanoi for the first time. The unit debuted the 3000-lb M118 Low Drag General Purpose bomb 17 days later when it attacked the bridge at Thanh Hoa. Once again, serious damage was caused but no spans were dropped. Better results were achieved with the weapon on 10 August when the 12th TFS destroyed the Vinh Tuy bridge near Dien Bien Phu. Thirteen days later the US government allowed a one-off raid to be made on the otherwise forbidden dams and locks of the country's hydroelectric network. Eight M118s were dropped on the Ban Thach plant on a day when 228 tons of bombs fell on North Vietnam.

The Vinh Tuy mission also saw the first use of the AGM-12C Bullpup B missile by F-105s. With its 1000-lb warhead rather than the 570-lb version fitted to the AGM-12B, the revised Bullpup could be fired at a distance of up to ten miles away from the target. Once the weapon was in the air, the pilot steered it using flares on the missile's cruciform tail as a visual reference. Whilst the AGM-12B could be fired straight off the fighter's pylon, the C-model had to be dropped and then fired via a frangible cable. The hazards of this process were apparent when Capt J R Mitchell of the 421st TFS fired one on 27 July 1966. The missile did not release properly from its pylon's front shackle, canted tail-down, fired and caused severe damage as it shot through the leading edge of the F-105's wing. The pilot ejected when his Thunderchief (61-0045) drained the last of its hydraulic fluid and crashed five miles from the forward recovery base at Nakhon Phanom.

Jack Broughton's experience of the Bullpup was not uncommon;

'The only memory I have of the missile is firing it, then watching it rock and roll through the sky heading nowhere close to what I had aimed at, with a pretty good assurance that it would hit the surface . . . someplace.'

A further problem with the AGM-12 was that NVA gunners learned to fire into its smoke trail, knowing that a guiding F-105 was close behind.

SAM WARS

Because the Johnson administration forbade an all-out assault on the SA-2 SAM sites that had become active in North Vietnam on 23 July 1965, it was vital to find the technology to help pilots defeat this new, potent, threat. The QRC-160-1 electronic countermeasures (ECM) pod had been trialled initially in April 1965 on the RF-101C photo-reconnaissance aircraft, but aerodynamic vibration prevented its effective use. Although SAMs shot down their first US aircraft on 24 July, no F-105s were actually lost to an SA-2 until 30 September.

The first 9th TRS RB-66C and EB-66E Destroyers also arrived in-theatre in April to provide radar jamming. They were joined by four RB-66Bs and six more RB-66Cs at Tan Son Nhut on 6 April 1965. These jets first detected emissions from the SA-2's 'Fan Song' radar during an F-105 mission on 24 July, thus beginning a long 'battle of the radar waves' with Soviet SAM technicians. RB-66Bs were initially used as *Brown Cradle* pathfinders for F-105 formations. This technique was established informally via conversations between F-105 pilot Capt Bob Green and RB-66 crewmen Capts Charles Schaufler and Bill Mahaffey. On *Brown Cradle* missions in poor visibility, an RB-66B would lead flights of F-105s, possibly accompanied by B-57s and F-4s, using its K-5 bombing/navigation equipment (better than that fitted to any of these tactical jets). The RB-66 navigator gave the fighter-bombers a radio 'heads-up' prior to the bomb run and then a ten-second tone on their headsets. When the tone stopped, all aircraft dropped in unison. This tactic worked well against targets that gave a recognisable radar return.

Although the F-105's AN-131 Doppler system was advanced for its time, it was not designed for the tough Southeast Asian climate. Col Jack Broughton recalled;

'I believe that the Dopplers didn't care for the humidity, dirt and rough rides they had to endure. I also believe they had a fear of combat, since they usually quit about the time you entered the hot area of the North.'

The first mission was flown with 16 F-105s led by Capt Jeremy Grimes' RB-66, with a second run leading 12 F-105s to drop their 60 M117s on Vinh harbour. *Brown Cradle*-led missions were replaced by *Combat Skyspot* from May 1966.

Although North Vietnam's integrated air defence system was still in its infancy in respect to the threat posed by SAMs in the summer of 1965, the communists' ever-increasing AAA strength was beginning to exact a real toll on the F-105 force both north of the DMZ and in Laos. Ten Thunderchiefs were downed in May and June, but 27 July brought the worst ordeal of that summer.

Five active SA-2 sites had been established by then, and their first victim was a Ubon-based 15th TFW F-4C hit on 24 July. The US government was apparently 'surprised' that the missile had been fired,

having assumed that SAMs had been intended merely as a threat. A reprisal attack was sanctioned, Adm Sharp hastily ordering *Spring High* to be flown on 27 July. This mission would be performed by 48 F-105s armed with CBU-2s, napalm and rockets. Eleven jets would target SAM Site 6, 12 would hit Site 7 and 23 others would bomb the SA-2 operators' barracks. Eight more Thunderchiefs were tasked with flak suppression, as 37 mm, 57 mm and 85 mm AAA batteries surrounded the SAM sites.

The attackers dropped their ordnance in line-abreast flights of four at a height of just 50-100 ft. The first flight immediately took hits, and the 563rd TFS's Capt Walt Kosko went down in F-105D 62-4257 and drowned in the Black River near Site 7 – he had survived being shot down (in 61-0133) during a SAR mission over Laos on 5 June. A follow-up attack on the same site (which later proved to be empty) an hour later cost a second aircraft, Capt Kile Berg, also of the 563rd TFS, becoming a PoW after 61-0113 was hit on a napalm pass. At Site 6, Capt William Barthelmas' 61-0177 from the 357th TFS was hit as it left its target. The pilot had almost made it back to Ubon RTAFB when his aircraft became uncontrollable, tragically colliding with its escort F-105D (62-4298). In the ensuing crash, Barthelmas and Maj Jack Farr in the second jet were both killed, although their loss was officially listed as an 'operational accident' so as to avoid publicity linking Thailand to *Rolling Thunder*.

Another F-105D (62-4407) in the 'mop-up' 'Dogwood' flight, charged with destroying anything that had been left by the main force, was hit by AAA as it avoided a volley of SAMs. Pilot Capt Frank Tullo of the 12th FS was the only aviator to be rescued that day. A newly deployed HH-3 staging through the secret *Lima* Site 36 in Laos flew further into North Vietnam than any previous SAR helicopter and retrieved Tullo. Squadronmate Capt Robert Purcell was less fortunate. Hit by flak attacking the SAM barracks, he ejected from 62-4252 and was captured.

The loss of six F-105s on a single mission was clearly unsustainable, and better tactics were needed to avoid the flak and the SAMs. The highly mobile SA-2 launchers which, in the words of 2nd Air Division CO Gen Joseph Moore, 'had precluded medium-altitude air operations', could be moved in a few hours. This in turn made it almost impossible to determine which sites were active, rather than just 'dummys' or carefully

SITTING PRETTY carries a load of M117s, an unusual serial presentation and the remains of a yellow nose band, suggesting previous ownership by the 12th TFS at Korat. Its pilot, Capt H W Moore, was among a number of F-105 aircrew who appeared to have ejected safely, but were never heard from again. 61-0078 was struck by ground fire as Moore dived on the Xom Cul bridge on 3 September 1967 (*Don Larsen*)

contrived flak-traps. With the latter, batteries of 37 mm to 57 mm guns were focused on a set point and altitude from which aircraft had to begin their bomb runs, often at the top, or 'perch', of a 'pop-up' to the roll-in dive-to-attack point, or at a predictable point as the F-105 pulled up from its attack. These 'firing cells' could put 1000+ rounds into a 'box' of airspace in less than five seconds. To catch fighters at lower altitudes 'barrage fire' was used, with hundreds of small arms or small-calibre AAA firing a curtain of bullets through which the fighter would have to pass.

The North Vietnamese played the same trick on 9 August when Maj James Hosmer of the 12th TFS led an attack by three flights of CBU-carrying F-105s on the newly discovered SAM Site 8 near Hanoi. Eight more jets followed the initial strike up with M117s. Hosmer received a Silver Star for a well-executed attack, although the site was empty.

A new anti-SAM strategy was developed from these attacks using the Pacific Command nickname *Iron Hand*, which had initially been used for US Navy A-4 and A-6A flak suppression missions. Starting with a 16 August attack on Binh Linh, USAF strike missions now had a dedicated quick-reaction flight of *Iron Hand* F-105s that could be despatched on all missions to find and destroy SAM sites. Sadly, few of the latter were located that summer (as McNamara noted disparagingly), and the missile launch vehicles' mobility allowed a SAM, initially thought to have been the more advanced SA-3, to be fired at a returning F-105 strike close to the Laotian border on 9 September.

Site attacks intensified, and on 16 September Lt Col Robbie Risner's luck finally ran out when he led an *Iron Hand* flight against a site near the fabled Thanh Hoa bridge. A week previously he had used different tactics and flown as the only flak suppressor aircraft in his flight. His jet took a head-on hit as he released his bombs in a carefully coordinated low altitude attack on the Yen Khaoi army base by the 67th TFS. Risner's canopy was blown off and a piece of red-hot shrapnel burned his shoulder and stabbed itself into his seat headrest. Risner, stuck with his open-top 'Thud', tanking successfully from a KC-135 before returning to base.

For the 16 September mission he put himself on the 0900 hrs *Iron Hand* launch in place of another pilot, briefed over breakfast and took off with two flights that split into two-ship elements nearer the target. His aircraft (F-105D 61-0217) carried napalm for the 'Fan Song' radar unit and

his wingman, Mike Stevens, had M117s, which were to be dropped on the site from an afterburner climb and dive attack. They approached the target so low that Risner had to climb to avoid a 100 ft hill, at which point he was hit by AAA. Stevens alerted him to a raging fire in the main fuel tank, but Risner lit the afterburner, cleaned off his ordnance and headed for the coast at 550 knots. Only three miles from the water the hydraulics finally drained out, causing the control column to go full forward and the

Choking Thiokol cartridge-starter fumes start to billow from 62-4356 *MUMBLES* on the Korat ramp. The big cylindrical cartridge was ignited by the aircraft's battery, and it wound the engine up to 12 per cent revolutions, at which point the pilot pressed the 'start' button (*USAF*)

F-105 began an uncontrollable dive. Risner ejected and landed, with his 45-lb survival kit still attached to him, rather than swinging below on a lanyard, and he soon began a seven-year stretch as a PoW.

After several other similar occurrences where F-105s had crashed because they had lost all their hydraulic fluid, the jet was finally given an automatic lock to keep the stabilator in the neutral position. The aircraft could then fly straight and level when the hydraulics were hit, rather than diving earthward with the control column sometimes locked at an angle that could injure the pilot on ejection. Later still a more comprehensive fix introduced a third, back-up hydraulic system to give basic flight control. This was housed in a slim ridge fairing on the aircraft's spine.

Improvements in the aircraft's survivability in such an unexpectedly hostile environment were 'sorely needed and wanted', as Col Jack Broughton remembers, 'but fire retardant and a subsequent modification for protection from a violent pitch-down after complete loss of hydraulic pressure that could preclude safe ejection remained high on our wish list'. Fuel tanks were duly made self-sealing and lined with fire-retardant polyurethane foam, while fuel feed lines received better protection.

F-105 units also had to urgently embrace anti-SAM measures. On 23 September, for example, pilots used the hair-raising 'SAM break' tactic for the first time. This involved watching the missile and turning towards it, before breaking away at the last moment to defeat its radar lock. Help was also on the way in the form of ECM additions to the aircraft. The US Navy had already experienced some success in the use of AN/ALQ-51 devices to break the 'Fan Song' radar's missile lock, defeating six SAMs with the system on 16 September.

Despite the introduction of these measures, on 30 September the first Thunderchief was lost to a SAM when F-105D 61-0117, piloted by 334th TFS CO Lt Col Melvin Killian, was hit while orbiting over the Ninh Binh bridge target at 18,000 ft. The aircraft began to burn fiercely and exploded moments later, killing its pilot.

Another US Navy initiative in the form of the Texas Instruments AGM-45 Shrike anti-radiation missile was tested in combat from August 1965, A-4 Skyhawks achieving just two 'probable' hits with the weapon in 25 launches. The missile had to be pre-tuned to a known radar frequency before launch, and fired at a distance of just five miles from the target. Its seeker head presented target data to the F-105 pilot as audio tones that were linked to the aircraft's attitude indicator, using the pitch and bank steering bars to present directional cues for launching the missile. SA-2 operators soon learned that switching their 'Fan Song' or 'Fire Can' units to standby mode upon detecting a Shrike launch broke the missile's lock.

Attempting to make 'Fan Song' transmit long enough to fix its position via an RB-47 electronic reconnaissance aircraft, 12 F-105s flew with a Ryan 147D drone

A 37 mm shell punched this hole through the tail of Col Broughton's *Alice's Joy* when he strafed six trucks during his return flight from a Viet Tri railway marshalling yard strike. By pulling a circuit breaker to neutralise the damaged and wildly oscillating automatic stabilisation system, and slowing the F-105 down so that the fin was not ripped off, the highly experienced Broughton managed to nurse the aircraft home (*Col Jack Broughton*)

F-105Ds shared the *Iron Hand* mission with F-100Fs and F-105Fs from early 1966. 58-1161 of the 469th TFS is seen here in May 1966 armed with an AGM-45 Shrike. Six months later on 22 November 1966, the jet's engine lost power, possibly after AAA damage, as it climbed away from its target. At the time the aircraft carried two QRC-160 pods, and as its pilot managed to coax the Thunderchief over the Thai border before ejecting, a search party was sent to recover the pods. A new pod was made from the remains, and it achieved record reliability rates (*USAF via Chris Hobson*)

(a favourite SA-2 target) ahead of their formation on 31 August. The drone successfully tracked the location of three emission sources before being shot down, but when the F-105s closed in to attack the batteries, they were still unable to identify the well-camouflaged sites visually, losing a 67th TFS F-105D (61-0185) over their secondary bridge target.

Using a different strategy on 31 October, eight Korat-based *Iron Hand* 562nd TFS F-105s were led on a mission by Cdr Richard Powers, Operations Officer of VA-164, embarked in USS *Oriskany* (CVA-34). Powers' 'pathfinder' A-4E carried an early Sanders AN/ALQ-51 defensive electronic counter-measures (DECM) set. While 65 US Navy aircraft hit a bridge near Kep airfield, the F-105s bombed a nearby SAM site. The DECM equipment detected 'Fan Song' emissions from one site and Powers saw two missiles launched from a second. He targeted the F-105s for 600-knot pop-up attacks against the second one and ran in for a Snakeye bomb attack on the first at 150 ft. Powers' Skyhawk took several AAA hits and he ejected, but was not heard from again. The F-105s took out a third active site with M117s before leaving. Powers' DECM set had helped the raiders avoid being hit by any of the 28 SA-2s fired at them. Indeed, the only damage was caused by the premature detonation of a 20 mm round in one of the F-105s' M61A1 guns.

Clearly, DECM could reduce the SAM threat, but it would be a while before the USAF could field such equipment for its own aircraft. Meanwhile, losses continued, including a third squadron commander. On 5 November Lt Col George McCleary of the 357th TFS was leading an *Iron Hand* strike on the SAM-support area at Guoi Bo, which was weather-aborted. Diverting to an armed reconnaissance instead, he was hit in cloud by an SA-2. McCleary appeared to have ejected from F-105D 62-4342, but after a fruitless SAR attempt he was listed as killed in action.

A 469th TFS *Iron Hand* Thunderchief (62-4332) was lost to an SA-2 during the newly deployed unit's first combat mission on 16 November, Capt Don Green dying when the aircraft crashed in the sea. Further underlining the hazards associated with the *Iron Hand* mission, the unit lost a second F-105D (61-0062) to AAA as it hunted for SAM sites near the Laotian border just 48 hours later. Capt Larry Mahaffey was rescued and an SA-2 site was hit by numerous 2.75-inch rockets in a 'pop-up' attack from low altitude by the rest of his flight.

Bridge attacks had also continued throughout this period, with the US government releasing more targets for *Rolling Thunder 34-47* – the latter ended with a 36-day pause from 24 December. Eighteen F-105s dropped a span of the Long Het bridge with M118s on 5 October, but two jets from the 36th TFS were lost to AAA. Maj Dean Pogreba, previously downed on 22 August, headed north (in F-105D 62-4295) and ejected over China, where he may have been imprisoned. Had he returned, he could have faced a court martial for attacking an incomplete (therefore 'off limits') SAM site the previous day. Pogreba's fate remains a mystery. Capt Bruce Seeber (in F-105D 62-4376) was captured close to the target.

On 17 October no fewer than 32 M118s were dropped on the Bac Can highway bridge without loss. Waterborne targets also came under attack as Hanoi switched some of its transport from roads to rivers.

15 December saw a target only 16 miles from Hanoi bombed when a series of raids on the Uong Bi thermal power station commenced. Twenty-three F-105s joined a 90-aircraft strike, though only seven could drop successfully as the target was obscured by unexpected cloud. Capt Harry Dewitt of the 334th TFS was the only casualty, the controls of F-105D 62-4363 locking solid as its hydraulic fluid leaked away following a 37 mm AAA hit. Dewitt ejected over the sea and broke his leg when he hit the water. He was quickly recovered by an HU-16B.

Two modifications to the operational routine occurred in late 1965. On 10 December North Vietnam was divided into six 'route packages' by Adm Sharp. Initially, the USAF and US Navy were to exchange 'packs' weekly, but since the latter's carrier-based jets preferred shorter flights to their targets they took on the coastal areas (Route Packages I, III and VIB, including Haiphong docks), while Thailand-based USAF units had longer, more exposed flights to Route Packages II, IV, V and VIA, the latter including Hanoi, Thai Nguyen and two MiG airfields.

The second change, to PCS squadrons, was heralded by the arrival of the 354th and 333rd TFSs at Takhli in November and December, respectively, and a change in the definition of a tour of duty. Rather than brief TDYs, crews were now expected to remain for one year, or 100 missions – whichever happened soonest. As losses mounted, many pilots wondered if either was feasible. Indeed, the mindset of aviators flying the F-105 in Southeast Asia at the time was starkly revealed by the following popular wisdom that did the rounds at the Thai bases;

'The most optimistic man in the world is an F-105 jockey who gives up smoking because he's afraid of cancer.'

The 335th TFS/4th TFW conducted the advanced pre-service tests on both the B- and D-model F-105s in 1958 and 1960, respectively. It deployed to Yokota AB, Japan, on 3 July 1965 and thence to Takhli RTAFB on 3 November 1965. Nineteen days later, 62-4370 was photographed carrying six M117 bombs on a mission over the North. On 7 August 1966 – a day when five F-105s were lost – this jet was hit by a 100 mm shell shortly after conducting its bombing run on the POL storage facility at Thai Nguyen. 1Lt Michael Brazelton, who was on his 11th mission, ejected and was taken prisoner (*USAF*)

STRIKES AND LOSSES

As 1966 began Gen John McConnell increased air support for growing US Army activity in-theatre by deploying a further 16 TAC squadrons mainly to bases in South Vietnam, although he hoped that they could also fly *Rolling Thunder* missions too. He objected to the US government's 'gradualism', but other influential voices, notably Under Secretary of State George Ball, assured President Johnson that a major bombing assault on North Vietnam would trigger nuclear war with China within months. Nevertheless, *Rolling Thunder* proceeded, with 120 of the 300 daily sorties being flown by the USAF.

Bad weather cancelled all missions until 31 January, when an armed reconnaissance destroyed some barges but cost F-105D 61-0210 and the life of its 469th TFS pilot, Capt Gene Hamilton. Four other F-105s had been lost that month in Laotian operations, two through engine failure.

While the poor weather continued, more than 95 percent of F-105 missions over the North were led by RB-66B/C *Brown Cradle* pathfinders that also jammed radar-controlled AAA. Major strikes in the Mu Gia 'bottleneck' and Barthelmy pass were made in this way too, as were three attacks on Dien Bien Phu airfield in early February. Operations in *Rolling Thunder 48/49* from February to early May were still inhibited by monsoon weather. *Rolling Thunder 50* enlarged the battlefield area, but mainly into the 'panhandle' of Laos for infiltration route interdiction. The 12th annual request by JCS for attacks on MiG airfields was rejected, as were repeated demands to destroy the large SA-2 store holding 130 missiles at Gia Thong Boe.

A 13-aircraft F-105 strike was possible on 29 April when the Thai Nguyen railway marshalling yard sustained major damage, temporarily slowing supplies to the USAF's preferred target, the huge local steel mill. Only one F-105 went down during the mission, 1Lt Donald Bruch's 333rd TFS jet (62-4304) being damaged by an 85 mm shell. Having flown 20 miles to the north-west of Thai Nguyen, it dived uncontrollably into the ground with Bruch still in the cockpit.

The Johnson administration did approve re-strikes on repaired bridges, and these were particularly hazardous. Six days prior to the Thai Nguyen mission, two 421st

The wrecked airbrake and vertical stabiliser components of F-105D-15-RE 61-0051, shot down by an SA-2 on 24 April 1966. Lt Col William Cooper, commander of the 469th TFS/388th TFW, was leading an attack on the Phu Lang Thuong bridge in this aircraft when it was hit by the SAM, the pilot losing his life as the aircraft disintegrated around him (*via Istvan Toperczer*)

62-4347 soaks up the midday sun in a 333rd TFS revetment at Takhli. In February 1984 62-4347 was retired to a pylon at Hill AFB as the 'High Time Thud', serving as a memorial to all personnel who lost their lives flying the F-105 (*USAF*)

TFS F-105Ds were shot down while bombing the Phu Lang Thuong road bridge on the route to China. Capt Robert Dyczkowski's aircraft (61-0157) took a hit on his 99th mission on egress from the target and he could not eject. In the following flight 15 minutes later, Maj Bernard Goss was hit in 61-0048 and ejected, but was killed whilst being captured.

Twenty-four hours later, a re-strike of the target was ordered, and two more F-105s were lost. 469th TFS CO Lt Col William Cooper died when his fighter (61-0051) was intercepted by an SA-2, and squadronmate 1Lt Jerry Driscoll was downed when his jet (62-4340) burst into flames after suffering a 57 mm AAA hit. Driscoll, who was flying his 112th mission, ejected and was captured. He spent seven years in prison, suffering the ritual public humiliation that several F-105 pilots were forced to endure.

The ongoing 'war of the bridges' also required five Thunderchief missions against the Bac Giang bridge, a massive structure on the northeast railway to China. Twenty-six F-105s with M117 bombs

Maintenance personnel from Da Nang's 388th TFW 'Gunfighters' contemplate the 'tail-less wonder' – an F-105D (possibly 58-1167) with its right stabiliser shot away (*via Col Jack Broughton*)

initially caused only minor damage to the steel and concrete, but on a fifth mission with 3000-lb bombs by eight jets on 5 May the two northern spans were collapsed, partly by a hit from mission leader Capt C Glen Nix. On the same mission 1Lt Karl Richter, nearing the 200-mission mark in his second tour, had closed on another F-105 at low altitude as it unexpectedly jettisoned its two massive M118s. He flew directly over the blast, which blew off his F-105's right stabilator and holed the rear fuselage, but the tough fighter maintained hydraulic pressure and got him back to Korat.

The previous day another 34th TFS pilot had bombed a target near Dong Hoi, but one of his two 3000-lb bombs hung up, throwing the unbalanced F-105D into a hard right inverted dive at low altitude. He went with the right-hand roll rather than trying to correct it and managed to pull out and jettison the weighty weapon.

The monsoon began to ease late in May after 40 per cent of that month's Thunderchief sorties had been cancelled. One of the year's biggest operations involved all F-105 units in a 31 May attack on the Yen Bay military storage area, destroying 72 warehouses and damaging 40 others, plus many AAA positions. Two jets were lost to AAA, however, 1Lt Leonard Ekman of the 354th TFS (in 62-4386) being downed by an 85 mm shell during the first wave attack mounted by the Takhli wing. He ejected and was rescued by an HH-3E on one of the deepest SAR penetrations of the war to date. Capt Martin Steen of the 469th TFS (in 61-0120) was not so lucky when the Korat wing attacked Yen Bay 30 minutes later. Ejecting near to Ekman, Steen landed in mountainous terrain and disappeared. His harness was later found by a SAR Pararescue Jumper, but there was no sign of Steen.

Losses mounted as Route Pack VIA missions increased, and the pilots' chances of survival were diminished by fearsome AAA defences and little hope of recovery in such hostile territory. By April 1966 F-105 missions were four times more likely to be fired on than in December 1965, and

Seen on 13 May 1966, 60-0421 *THE GREAT PUMPKIN* from the 469th TFS wears the letter 'P' (for Pumpkin) on its fin as part of an experimental identification code system that was later replaced by formal two-letter tail codes. Hit in the left wing by SA-2 shrapnel during a 14 May 1967 attack on the Ha Dong barracks, the jet (by then with the 13th TFS) got its pilot, Maj J R Wilson, to within five miles of the Laotian border before he ejected and was rescued (*Don Larsen*)

58-1167 *MISS UNIVERSE* of the 34th TFS taxies out at Korat in May 1967 at the start of a functional check flight. There is evidence that the jet has had a replacement fin fitted from a reverse-camouflage aircraft, as well as other repairs to the rear fuselage. 58-1167 had its right stabiliser shot away during a mission over the North, but its pilot managed to fly the F-105 back to Da Nang, where it made an emergency landing (*D Larsen via Norm Taylor*)

there were 14,000 known AAA sites in place by then, with 115 SAM sites by July 1966. Enemy 85 mm AAA was effective up to 14,000 ft, 57 mm between 5000-6000 ft (both 'Firecan' radar controlled) and innumerable optically-aimed 37 mm guns waited for aircraft at lower altitude.

Following the loss of nine F-105s in April and 14 in May, a further 11 jets were downed during June, all bar two of them to AAA. Things got worse in July, when a staggering 19 Thunderchiefs were destroyed. Included in this total were the first two *Wild Weasel* F-105Fs to be lost in combat. The lowest point in a bad month had come on 11 July, when three F-105Ds from the 355th TFW were shot down. Two of them (62-4282 and 61-0112) were hit by AAA during an attack on the Vu Chua railway bridge, and a third (61-0121) crashed due to fuel exhaustion after tangling with a MiG-17. Only one pilot, Capt Lewis Shattuck, was captured after ejecting for the second time in eleven days.

August provided no respite for F-105 crews with 18 jets lost, followed by 13 in September. Such attrition could not be sustained for long.

POL

A number of the jets lost in the spring and summer of 1966 had been attacking North Vietnam's vital petroleum, oil and lubricant (POL) supplies. With the vast increase in truck traffic on the trails heading south, the demand for fuel grew accordingly, and the North looked to foreign sources such as the Soviet Union to satisfy its needs.

The US government hesitantly sanctioned attacks on the huge underground fuel storage tanks at seven sites around Hanoi in June, with missions commencing on the 29th of that month when a 16-strong F-105 package, two *Iron Hand* flights, 24 F-4Cs and an F-104 CAP targeted the POL facilities. A 388th TFW strike package of 34th and 421st TFS F-105s, led by Lt Col James Hopkins, struck first from the south. They devastated 90 per cent of a POL tank farm three miles from Hanoi with 188 M117s, leaving a smoke column that rose to 35,000 ft.

The second strike of the day was led by Maj James Kasler, who was also the 354th TFS operations officer. His jets came in along the north side of

By mid-1967 F-105 wings were mounting two morning and two afternoon 'mission packages' daily, each with around 100 strike and support aircraft. Participating in just such a mission, flight lead aircraft 62-4361/JJ was initially delivered to the 8th TFW in 1963. Transferred to the 388th TFW in 1966, it had accumulated 2927 combat hours by 30 June 1969. The fighter completed its combat period with the 44th TFS at Takhli in October 1970 and then spent more than eight years with the Kansas ANG's 184th TFG, before finally joining the 465th TFS (*USAF*)

the 5000-ft mountain range north of Hanoi known as 'Thud Ridge' because the remains of many shot-down F-105s lay there. This provided cover until the final 25-mile stretch to Hanoi. The RoE then forced Kasler to overfly Hanoi and attack from the south in case a 'long' bomb should accidentally fall in the centre of the North Vietnamese capital. He subsequently reported;

'Approaching from the north, we had to make a 180-degree pop-up manoeuvre to strike the target as ordered. What the attack order meant was that every aircraft would be rolling into the bomb run at approximately the same spot, heading in the same direction. Not too smart from the pilots' viewpoint, but in the interests of protecting civilian populations such orders were commonplace in Vietnam.'

Only one pilot suffered for this lack of divergent attack headings. The F-105s approached at a height of only 300 ft, and the 85 mm and 100 mm AAA guns around the city had to fire at almost flat trajectories. Capt Murphy Jones' F-105D (60-0460) took an 85 mm shell hit on his second attack and the 333rd TFS pilot ejected close to Gia Lam airport. Jones, who was on his third tour of duty, suffered a spinal fracture, a broken arm and serious shrapnel wounds to his leg. Nevertheless, he was bundled into the back of a truck and humiliated in a 'Hanoi march' public parade.

The 355th TFW attack destroyed most of the 32 main fuel tanks containing 17 per cent of North Vietnam's reserves, and it was described by the Seventh Air Force as 'the most significant and important strike of the war' so far. For good measure, Maj Jim 'The Destroyer' Kasler, who always made a point of expending all of his ammunition on each sortie, found 25 trucks in the open on a new road east of Hanoi and raked 18 with gunfire. He was awarded the Air Force Cross for leading the mission.

On 29 June the officer in charge of defending Hanoi had held back his SAM batteries (which, Kasler later deduced, had cost him his job), but they contributed to the massive barrage that greeted the following day's raids on POL sites at Thai Nguyen and Viet Tri by two formations of 12 F-105s. These attacks were not so effective, destroying less than 20 per cent of their targets. One 388th TFW F-105D (62-4224) was lost, although its pilot, Capt R K Nierste, ejected safely after a 200-mile flight in his damaged Thunderchief.

Despite these attacks, supplies of fuel continued unabated through Haiphong docks, and the US government still rejected the bombing or mining of this crucial facility. The Johnson administration also kept other key POL targets 'off limits' too, which meant that they had to be struck piecemeal. In the wake of these strikes, the North Vietnamese began to disperse fuel reserves, hiding drums alongside roads and rivers.

In October 1966 McNamara told President Johnson that the POL campaign had done nothing to alter the mindset in Hanoi, and to him it

Champagne for four pilots from the 388th TFW, namely Capts Bruce Holmes (who died in a house fire near McConnell AFB in January 1967) and William May from the 469th TFS, and Capts Richard Ely and William Ramage of the 421st TFS, upon the completion of their 100th missions on 15 January 1966. When Col Broughton became Vice Commander of the 355th TFW in June 1966, the average age of the pilots was 38. They were highly experienced, and often held masters' degrees or doctorates. Several went on to complete 200 F-105 missions. Their 'new guy' replacements from early 1967 onwards often lacked fighter experience, however (*USAF*)

was additional proof that bombing the North would never win the war. Many others felt that it was obvious that the POL 'tap' should have been turned off at Haiphong at the start of hostilities.

By then Maj Jim Kasler had been languishing in a Hanoi prison for two months, his jet being one of eleven F-105D/Fs lost in the first eight days of August. Kasler, who was taking part in his 91st *Rolling Thunder* mission, was downed by AAA whilst attacking a warehouse complex northwest of Hanoi. His 354th TFS flight had already dropped CBU-2/As from 200 ft, and seen many solid hits, when they went after a secondary supply depot with their remaining ordnance. As they pulled off-target, Kasler's wingman, 1Lt Fred Flom, took a 37 mm AAA hit in the belly of his F-105D (62-4327), and on his leader's advice he ejected at 550 knots at an altitude of 1000 ft. Seconds later the fighter exploded and Flom landed unconscious only 55 miles from Hanoi.

Kasler took his flight to a tanker to refuel, and then returned for RESCAP duties, but Flom had already been captured. While orbiting above the crash site, Kasler's F-105D (62-4343) was hit twice by a 57 mm battery and the cockpit filled with smoke. His unmodified hydraulic system ran down, leaving ejection as his only option, but the control column locked against his right knee, pushing it against the canopy rail as the seat shot him from the crippled jet, causing a dreadful leg fracture. The former World War 2 B-29 tail-gunner and six-kill MiG ace from the Korean War was captured, spending six years as a PoW.

Impenetrable weather covered much of North Vietnam in the winter of 1966-67, but the losses continued, albeit at a rate of only 1.6 per 1000 sorties – an indication of the F-105s' workload. Five jets were lost in October, nine in November and seven in December. Of these, one of the most severe blows was the death of yet another squadron commander in the form of Lt Col Don Asire, the highly regarded CO of the 354th TFS, on 8 December.

The 355th TFW had been sent to bomb railway and POL targets near

The crackling roar of a J75 rends the air as F-105D 60-0449 *007* winds up for take-off at Korat. Also known as *Bounty Hunter*, *The Blue Fox* and *Jose Shillelagh*, this aircraft served with the Virginia ANG in the 1970s (*USAF*)

An early prototype laser-guided bomb (LGB) with steerable tail fins, tested on an F-105 during *Rolling Thunder*. Thunderchiefs flew 113 sorties against the Thanh Hoa bridge in 1966-68, facing 300+ AAA guns and 109 SA-2 missiles. On 13 May 1972 the colossal bridge was finally dropped by F-4s armed with Paveway I LGBs (*USAF*)

Phuc Yen but they were 'weathered out', so the strike force turned to its secondary target. With MiG and SAM warnings blaring in their headsets, 'Kingpin' flight, led by Col Jack Broughton, with Lt Col Asire as his No 3, was attacked by four MiG-21s from the 921st FR. The VPAF jets had been vectored onto them from beneath the cloud-base by GCI, and they popped up through the overcast ready to launch their missiles.

Seeing that the secondary target was also obscured by cloud, Col Broughton ordered the two leading F-105 flights to jettison their bombs, light afterburner and turn to repel the MiGs. His own flight was actually behind the VPAF fighters at this point in the engagement, and the MiG pilots decided to break off their high-speed pursuit so as not to fall victim to the trailing 'Kingpin' jets. However, a single grey-camouflaged MiG-21 (allegedly flown by Russian 'advisor' Snr Lt Vadim Shchbakov) swooped down from above 'Kingpin' flight in pursuit of Lt Col Asire (in F-105D 59-1725) and his wingman, Hal Bingaman, who were accelerating ahead at 600 knots beneath the cloud cover, several thousand feet below 'Kingpin 1' and '2'. Shortly afterwards a wailing beeper marked the death-knell of Asire's jet, which had either been hit by an 'Atoll' missile (although the 921st FR made no claims) or AAA while the CO of the 354th FS tried to escape 'on the deck' at supersonic speed.

Planning and targeting for F-105 missions throughout *Rolling Thunder* was micro-managed from Washington, D.C. by the Johnson administration, but some tactical decisions were made locally. A December 1966 tactics conference at Ubon RTAFB proposed compressing the standard five-minute gaps between strike flights to make the defenders' task harder. However, that resolution went back to HQ Seventh Air Force and apparently stayed in someone's in-tray. Jack Broughton recalled;

'Nobody ever hung around waiting for some magic interval on any strike I led. I usually took the lead flight in on flak suppression and expected my flights to get in, do their job and get out of there. Somehow, any HQ-directed intervals must have escaped our notice. USAF, PACAF and Seventh and Thirteenth Air Forces all assumed they were controlling the details of our combat strikes. When you are hanging the collective asses of a lot of good guys all the way out over the fiercest defences in the history of military aviation, you pay little heed to the egos of those non-combat individuals from far, far away.'

The last two F-105s lost in combat in 1966 were downed during attacks on the Yen Vien railway marshalling yard. 61-0187, flown by Capt Samuel Waters of the 421st TFS, was the first go when it was hit by a SAM on 13 December as it climbed out from its bomb-run.

Col Jack Broughton's F-105D 62-4388 *Alice's Joy* is in the foreground of this view, having already replenished its tanks. After getting Broughton home on several occasions despite severe damage, the fighter was lost on 2 September 1967 when its pilot, Maj Will Bennett, hit a karst ridge and was killed after 62-4388 suffered flak damage. The silver 'Thud', 59-1731, was later camouflaged and became *The Frito Bandito* with the 355th TFW. At full thrust an F-105 burned 150 gallons of JP-4 per minute. Just to maintain altitude with a full bomb-load required 95 per cent military power, or 600 gallons per hour (*USAF*)

The pilot flew on for a further 15 miles before the aircraft crashed. Waters did not survive. The following day it was the 357th TFS's turn to target Yen Vien, which on this occasion was being defended by MiG-21s.

Capt R B 'Spade' Cooley, flying 60-0502, was intercepted by Dong Van De's MiG-21, which followed the final flight of strikers off the target at low altitude and then climbed for a missile attack 40 miles south of Yen Vien. Cooley's element was impeded by the heavy combat camera pod carried by his wingman's jet, which slowed the latter aircraft down. To make matters worse, both pilots soon became separated, allowing the MiG to attack unnoticed. Capt Cooley's engine exploded when it was struck by an 'Atoll', the F-105 disintegrating seconds later. Managing to eject, Cooley was surprised to find that he was still holding the remains of the throttle in his left hand as he parachuted down onto a small hill 30 miles from Hanoi. Despite having suffered a fractured vertebra during the ejection, Cooley crawled into the undergrowth and hid until he was rescued by an HH-3E. The latter was escorted by four A-1s that held off North Vietnamese troops who got to within 50 ft of Cooley's position.

By January 1967 F-105 units had been flying *Rolling Thunder* missions for the better part of two years. Just how effective these sorties had been remained difficult to quantify. It was known that much of the population of Hanoi had been evacuated, and that many citizens who might have joined the insurrection in the south were retained for defensive tasks. Yet despite considerable damage to its transport infrastructure and industrial capacity, North Vietnamese resolve and faith in its leadership remained strong, and President Johnson's only alternative to abandoning the campaign was further escalation of *Rolling Thunder.*

For the F-105 wings, which had lost 126 jets in 1966, the operational patterns established in the previous two years continued, but at a higher pace, although they benefitted from better protection offered by F-105F *Wild Weasel* flights and the introduction of ECM pods later in 1967.

POD POWER

Twenty-five improved QRC-160A (later AN/ALQ-71) pods were ordered in mid-1966 for the Thai F-105 wings. Tougher than the 1965 test models, they contained jammers for the 'Fan Song's' elevation and azimuth frequencies, as well as the 'Firecan' radar directing 57 mm and 85 mm AAA. From 26 September through to 8 October 1966, Project *Vampyrus* developed techniques for using these new pods, as evaluated by EB-66C crews. Various 'formations' were tried for maximum jamming protection, and initial combat results in late October showed that an 'echelon up from the leader' formation provided enough jamming power to prevent accurate guidance of both SA-2s and heavy flak.

Initially, two pods were carried on the F-105's outboard pylons covering all threat frequencies, but increased MiG activity required one to be replaced by an AIM-9B Sidewinder.

Brig Gen William Chairsell, commander of the 388th TFW, approved of the pods as they let F-105s make dive attacks from medium altitude, rather than 'popping up' in 30-degree, 4g climbs from lower altitude, where the jets were easier AAA targets. However, a 'Fan Song' could 'burn through' the pods emissions and lock onto an F-105 inside eight miles' range. The pod's effectiveness was also reduced while the jet was turning

or banking beyond 15 degrees, directing its radiation away from the radar it sought to blanket. Pods could also interfere with Shrike guidance and with the F-105's own RHAW system. A 'battle of the beams' began in which both sides constantly changed tactics, frequencies and formations.

A particular hazard for the F-105s was 'passive tracking' where the NVA 'triangulated' data from a number of sites and launched missiles at a point calculated to be the centre of the attack formation. Later in 1967 the improved AN/ALQ-87 (QRC-160-8) pod that could jam both the SA-2's position beacon and 'Fan Song' was introduced.

The 355th TFW approach to 'pod' formations differed from the Korat tactics, which relied on very close formations attacking from between 15,000 ft and 18,000 ft, with about two minutes between the formations. This placed them above the lighter AAA, although tight formations and relatively high altitudes limited the manoeuvrability of loaded F-105s against SAMs and MiGs. Jack Broughton explained;

'At Takhli we liked the pop-up tactic as we felt we got better target coverage with less exposure and fewer losses. Lots of folks agreed until new PACAF C-in-C Gen John D Ryan arrived in Honolulu with his high-altitude, straight-and-level B-17 experience and his SAC bomber philosophy. He directed a study that produced the phoniest untrue results possible, and despite much wailing from the veterans of the Hanoi environment, he ordered us to adopt the bomber approach. He seemed to feel the advent of ECM pods would solve all the problems up North, which they did not do. We continued to appeal our case, without much hope, but in the interim many of us never quite "understood" the General's direction, thus we did not get to fly the bomber patterns. We tried it one time and it was an obscene mess as far as we were concerned. The end of *Rolling Thunder* signalled the end of our attacks into RP VI, and therefore an end to that controversy.

'We liked to have as many pods as maintenance could provide, and we used them along with our pop-up tactic. Korat units liked that straight and level stuff, which may be why their loss rates were higher than ours and their bombs-on-target rates lower.'

'RYAN'S RAIDERS'

In an effort to circumvent the monsoon's annual decimation of *Rolling Thunder* missions, Gen Ryan asked for all-weather and night radar-bombing capabilities for the F-105 force to rival the US Navy's A-6A

61-0109 of the 333rd TFS eventually became the *Big Kahuna*, which was the nickname of 355th TFW boss Col John Giraudo, who led the wing from 2 August 1967 to 30 June 1968. The jet is seen here with a QRC-160 on the outboard pylon. Earlier versions of this 'quick reaction contract' ECM pod suffered a 60 per cent failure rate because its small generator propeller seized up at speed. Takhli's electronics troops modified it to run off the F-105's electrical system instead. In 1967 pods were so scarce that a C-47 was always sent to collect a pod from any F-105 that had to divert to another base. 61-0109 was shot down when its pilot, Maj Christos Bogiages (who was killed), made a fourth strafing run on a Plain of Jars target on 2 March 1969 (*USAF*)

60-0512 *THE MERCENARY* prepares to leave Korat's arming area in April 1967. Capt D K Thaete of the 34th TFS ejected from the jet after it was hit by AAA on 1 September 1968. He was rescued (*D Larsen/ Remington*)

F-105F 63-8285 served with the 44th TFS as a *Commando Nail* jet. Before take-off, the crew chief performed final walk-around checks after engine start and the pilot signalled 'remove chocks', tapping his brakes to check them as he began to taxi out. He also checked the stability augmentation system. The crew chief guided the aircraft out to the taxiway and saluted the crew on its way. After 'last chance' checks in the arming area, and a 'thumbs up' from the chaplain, the F-105 headed for the end of the runway. With canopies closed, the nose would dip as the J75 was run up. On brake release the afterburner cut in, emitting a 20-ft flame. Rings would appear in the plume of fire as the water injection added its extra thrust (*USAF via Chris Hobson*)

Intruder. Project *Bullseye* at Nellis AFB studied improving various tactical aircraft types, but an interim solution was attempted with Project *Northscope* in March 1967. Twenty-five pilots, including five *Wild Weasel* crews from the 41st AD at Yokota AB, were given additional training in all-weather bombing using F-105Fs from the *Wild Weasel III* conversion process that had carefully-tweaked R-14A radar (with fast scan and sector scan) and ASG-19 bombing systems. The 20 so-called 'Ryan's Raiders' F-105Fs, including eight without full *Wild Weasel* modifications, had a radar altimeter and a five-inch radar scope installed in the rear cockpit in place of the control column, armament panel, smaller radar scope and nuclear panel. They also had the ER-142 panoramic scan receiver and hard-to-read two-inch screen of the *Wild Weasel* fit.

The back-seater crews for these aircraft were rated pilots rather than electronic war officers (WSOs), as this reduced the amount of training they needed to perform the mission for they had already been taught low-altitude bombing – a necessity for penetrating North Vietnam beneath the country's extensive radar coverage. Jack Broughton recalled that 'the back-seater was responsible for punching off the ordnance'.

The first cadre of *Northscope* pilots formed part of the 13th TFS at Korat, but with their own commander in the form of Lt Col Fritz Treyz. Maj Bob Johnson flew the first *Northscope* mission on 26 April 1967 when he targeted the Yen Bai complex and the Ron ferry supply route. Over the next 80 days 98 sorties were flown against some of the most demanding targets in the North, and two jets were lost in May (63-8269 on the 12th and 62-4429 three nights later) and a third on the night of 4/5 October (63-8346). Four pilots were killed and two captured, and the October loss marked the end of 'Raider' operations over the North after 400+ sorties.

Normally, 'Raider' aircraft carried six M117s and two ECM pods or an AIM-9 (the latter were used to 'kill' two Chinese-operated searchlights during a mission involving Capts Jim Mirehouse and Mike

Michaels, with Maj Larry Friedman and Capt Tracy Rumsey in their back seats), and attack runs were made at around 1000 ft and 500 knots.

A further batch of *Wild Weasel*-trained crews took over the surviving 'Raider' aircraft in July 1967, alternating between Project *Commando Nail* night missions in RP I and *Wild Weasel* support for daytime strikes. High-altitude pathfinder missions (*Commando Nail Papa*) were added in July 1967, with two 'Raider' F-105Fs leading several flights of D-model jets that bombed in a timed sequence initiated by the 'Raider' crew. *Commando Nail* strikes continued until late October, when they merged with *Wild Weasel* missions. Their success established the framework for F-111A operations in-theatre the following year. Most surviving *Commando Nail* jets eventually reverted to F-105F/G configuration.

As part of Project *Combat Martin*, ten F-105Fs were modified with QRC-128 (later AN/ALQ-59) VHF communications jammers, used in the EB-66, to interrupt North Vietnamese ground-control conversations with MiG pilots. An AN/ALQ-55 communications jammer was also installed. AN/ALQ-59 equipment replaced the rear seat and instrument panel, while a large blade antenna appeared behind the rear cockpit. Several *Combat Martin* F-105Fs flew with the 355th and 388th TFWs, but only as single-seat bombers south of the DMZ for the AN/ALQ-59 was never officially cleared for use over the North. The seven surviving airframes were upgraded to F-105G specification in 1970.

Although these improvements were welcome, the basic *Rolling Thunder* missions changed very little. Indeed, the sortie rate intensified through 1967, and North Vietnam's defences became even more formidable. Particular areas such as Yen Bai became notoriously heavily defended hotspots, as Jack Broughton recalled;

'No place was worse than the 15-mile stretch of the northeast railway that ran between the Chinese buffer zone and the Hanoi "forbidden circle". Each of the two F-105 wings

63-8312 *Midnight Sun* was an early *Commando Nail* 13th TFS F-105F, and it is seen here at Korat on 23 June 1967. The aircraft was in a four-ship *Iron Hand* flight hitting a big Hanoi vehicle depot on 29 February 1968 when it took a SAM hit at 10,000 ft. Maj C J Fitton and Capt C S Harris ejected but neither of them survived (*Don Larsen*)

Lt Col Jack Spillers poses with his *Jeanie II* (62-4229), laden down with a load of Mk 82 LDGP bombs. Lt Col Spillers eventually completed a 114-mission tour with the 388th TFW, despite being shot down in 60-0516 during an *Iron Hand* flight on 26 March 1967. Evading capture in very hostile territory, he was rescued by an HH-3 helicopter whose crew made a hair-raising extraction. Returning to battle as commanding officer of the 357th TFS in 1969, Spillers flew a further 106 missions (*Jack Spillers via Norm Taylor*)

was forced to send a morning flight into the area on a daily basis to reconnoitre this desolate stretch of track. Every day the flights went at the same time, same altitude, same airspeed and same heading. The North moved every available gun into position along that track. There was never anything there except massive guns, whose concentration in mid-1967 averaged one gun every 18 ft.'

The target 'portfolio' did open up in February 1967, with the Thai Nguyen steelworks, a large cement factory in Haiphong and more of the country's power supply network all appearing on the approved list. Attacks on the massive steelworks began on 10 March with a memorable mission that saw the target badly damaged and 354th FS pilot Capt Max Brestel claim two MiG-17 kills. Despite these successes, it had been a hard mission for the unit nevertheless, as its 'Lincoln' flight had provided *Iron Hand* coverage for the strikers. Entering the intense 85 mm AAA ahead of the main force, the flight lost its lead jet, F-105F 63-8335, as it dived on a SAM site. Maj David Everson and Capt Jose Luna ejected and were taken prisoner. 'Lincoln 02' also took flak damage, but pilot Capt Bill Hoeft got the jet home with a four-feet diameter hole in its left wing.

Capts Merlyn Dethlefsen and Mike Gilroy in 'Lincoln 03' (F-105F 63-8341), also damaged by AAA, swung the second flight element around to re-attack the site amidst intense ground fire. Dethlefsen's wingman, Maj Ken Bell, then received an urgent warning about a MiG that was already firing at both 'Lincoln' jets. Gunfire damaged his right wing, making control difficult. The MiG-21 broke away when the F-105s were bracketed by another massive 85 mm barrage. In all, 'Lincoln 03' and '04' plunged through the flak and haze four times to attack and destroy two SAM sites. Dethlefsen was subsequently awarded the Congressional Medal of Honor for his gallant, unrelenting attack.

The following day the 355th TFW attacked the Thai Nguyen steelworks once again, and this time the wing lost three F-105Ds (60-0443, 62-4261 and 60-0506) in just four minutes to AAA and SAMs. Two of the pilots (Capt Charles Greene and Maj James Hiteshew) survived as PoWs, but the third (Capt Joseph Karins) was killed.

Rolling Thunder 55 was a belated response to more than two years of requests for permission to attack the MiGs' air bases. Hoa Lac and Kep were released for targeting, and eight F-105s from the 333rd TFS made the first attack on 24 April 1967, destroying 14 MiGs at Hoa Lac without loss. Further strikes by the 469th TFS took place in May. Eventually, all jet-capable bases were attacked apart from Gia Lam, near Hanoi, which was often used by Russian and Chinese civilian aircraft. Naturally, it became the main diversionary airfield for MiGs too.

Pilots often spoke of 'SAM days' or 'MiG days' after their missions, but it was hard to predict which they might meet as Col Broughton explained;

Maintenance continued around the clock to sustain the F-105 sortie rate during *Rolling Thunder*. Here, the 44th TFS's 60-0423 *Butterfly Bomber*, with a tarp over its nose to keep the monsoon rain out of its avionics bay, receives some attention to its AN/APR-25 antenna from Korat specialists in this March 1967 time-exposure photograph (*USAF*)

All three of these 355th TFW F-105Ds completed war service and established second careers. 61-0076, named *Cavalier* and *The Robin*, received Thunderstick II all-weather bombing system updates and joined the 457th TFS. 62-4361 *Christie, War Wagon* and *Blinky III*, among other nicknames, served with the 44th TFS through to 1969, then became *Yankee Peddler* with the Kansas ANG and was eventually put on display at Rickenbacker Air Base, Ohio. Finally, 59-1731 is seen here as *The Frito Bandito* (*USAF via Chris Hobson*)

'Higher headquarters had no knowledge of what we might expect. Wing Intelligence knew only what higher headquarters told them, thus "0+0=0". The first *Wild Weasels* into the area often got the first indication of what was ahead, and by the time the strike leader said "Clean 'em up, green 'em up and start your music" (clean up the cockpit and put away maps etc., activate armament switches and check for green "ready" lights and switch on ECM pods), we all knew for sure what kind of day it was.'

Six F-105s had been lost in January, two in February and ten in March, with the casualty rate rising as the weather improved and more missions were flown. April was to be a particularly bad month, with a dozen F-105s being destroyed. The first loss came on 2 April when Capt John Dramesi of the 13th TFS was shot down (in 60-0426) near Dong Hoi and captured after a brief small-arms duel with local militia. As a PoW, he initiated a series of escape attempts throughout his six years in captivity.

On 14 April Maj Paul Craw – described by veteran F-4 pilot Col Bob Ross as 'the toughest, hardest-nosed fighter pilot I have ever known' – was shot down in 357th TFS F-105D 60-0447 close to Dien Bien Phu, but despite severe injuries he was rescued in a rare, long-range HH-3 flight to the area. Two F-105 pilots with the same surname were lost on the same mission on 26 April, Capt William Meyer of the 469th TFS being shot down and killed in F-105D 58-1153 near Gia Lam airport, while Capt Al Meyer was captured after his 333rd TFS F-105F (piloted by the highly respected Maj John Dudash) took an SA-2 hit on an *Iron Hand* mission to Thai Nguyen, near Hanoi. Twenty-four hours earlier, in an equally cruel stroke of fate, 1Lt Robert Weskamp was killed during a 354th TFS attack on a Hanoi power station – a mission for which his brother's KC-135A had been one of the tankers. On 28 April Capt Franklin Karas was killed on a *Rolling Thunder* mission when his F-105D (58-1151) became the only victim of a MiG-21's guns, rather than missiles.

Finally, on 30 April, three 355th TFW F-105s were lost to MiG-21s in a mission against a thermal powerplant near Hanoi. The raid was led by Col

On 5 May 1967, F-105D 62-4401 of the 469th TFS was one of three Thunderchiefs lost in just ten minutes attacking the Ha Dong barracks. Part of 'Dagger' flight, it was hit by AAA at 17,000 ft, forcing Lt Col James Hughes to eject. His CO, World War 2 veteran Lt Col 'Swede' Larson, turned the mission into a SAR effort, but he too was shot down by an SA-2 missile, ejecting at around Mach 1. All three pilots lost on this mission were captured (*via Norm Taylor*)

60-0494 *Mr Pride* boasts one of the 469th TFS's distinctive identification symbols on its rudder. Air Force Crosses were awarded to HH-3E pilot Capt G Etzel and A-1 'Sandy' pilot Maj Larry Mehr for the parts they played in the rescue of Capt Dale Pichard of the 44th TFS, who was shot down in 60-0494 on 2 July 1967. He was forced to hide overnight in undergrowth adjacent to a well-used Ho Chi Minh trail route after his jet was hit by AAA near Xom Hoai (*Don Larsen*)

Jack Broughton, and in another remarkable coincidence two of the pilots downed shared the same surname – Capt Joseph and 1Lt Robert Abbott (in 61-0130 and 59-1726, respectively). As with Maj Leo Thorsness and Capt Harold Johnson (in *Wild Weasel* F-105F 62-4447), both Abbotts were captured.

Ten more Thunderchiefs went down in May, including three in ten minutes on the 5th near Hanoi. 1Lt James Shively of the 357th TFS ejected (from 61-1098) after being hit by AAA near the Yen Vien railway marshalling yard, and Lt Col James Hughes' 469th TFS jet (62-4401) took an 85 mm round in its tail, forcing him to eject also. His CO, Lt Col Gordon 'Swede' Larson, saw his wingman hit and turned away to escort him out. Having watched Hughes' canopy flutter away and his seat emerge, Larson initiated a RESCAP and accelerated back to the target area to rejoin his flight;

'I was in afterburner to increase my speed, and had just completed turning around when a tremendous explosion shook the aircraft. It was evident that a SAM had exploded with a proximity fuse towards the rear of my jet (62-4352). The jolt was tremendous. Indeed, it was so hard that it blew the glass faces off most of my instruments and threw up so much dust and debris that I could hardly see for several seconds. I was at about 4000 ft at the time, and in a slight dive. I pulled back on the stick to increase my altitude and found that it was like a limp noodle. I had no pitch control of my aircraft.'

After trying every way of inducing some pitch-up, including an attempt to extend the flaps and landing gear, 'Swede' Larson eventually ejected at 1000 ft and Mach 1.1, sustaining considerable injuries. He spent the rest of the war as a PoW.

Five Thunderchiefs went down in June, the first of these being lost on the 2nd when F-105D 61-0190 of the 34th TFS was hit by AAA at 16,000 ft as it ran in on the railway marshalling yards at Bac Giang.

Bursting into flames, the jet was abandoned by Maj Dewey Smith, who ejected into captivity.

Proof of the crippling nature of the RoE in-theatre for all US tactical aircraft came during the course of this mission. Returning from a successful bombing run, Maj Ted Tolman decided to deal with gun positions near the port of Cam Pha that had fired on his flight during

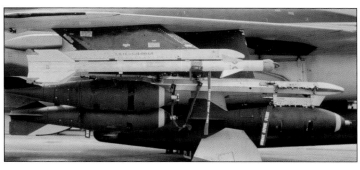

the outbound leg of the mission. As he strafed the gun-pits, Tolman saw a ship in the midst of the storm of AAA aimed at him. Unfortunately, it was the Russian freighter *Turkestan*, and high-level political protests ensued. These included a discussion between President Johnson and Soviet Premier Aleksei Kosygin during which the latter produced a 20 mm shell allegedly from the *Turkestan's* hull! These resulted in courts-martial for MiG killer Tolman, his wingman Maj Lonnie Ferguson and Vice Wing Commander Col Jack Broughton.

Tolman's flight had to weather-divert to Ubon, where he ill-advisedly stated that he had not fired his cannon during the mission. Out of loyalty to his pilots, Col Broughton helped to destroy Tolman's gun-camera film (used by the Seventh Air Force to monitor pilots' compliance to the RoE) on his return to Takhli. The two pilots were eventually acquitted, but Col Broughton, scheduled to assume command of the 432nd TRW at Udorn, was made the scapegoat. Relieved of his command, he left the service. Although a Washington, D.C. appeal court soon overturned the court-martial sentence as a gross miscarriage of justice, the USAF had already lost one of the most successful leaders of its F-105 operations. As Broughton put it, 'I had been shot down by our own people'.

Gen Ryan, instigator of the court-martial, was famous for his abrasiveness, as Broughton noted on another occasion involving F-105 cameras;

'"Thuds" had two cameras. The gun camera in the nose looked forward and was activated when the cannon or Sidewinders were fired. The sweep camera was mounted on the belly. It started running when the bombs were released and swept backwards to record their impact and provide good BDA. As you recovered from your steep dive-bombing run the sweep camera was registering bomb impact, and you jinked for your life or got shot down. Gen Ryan got these cameras and their functions mixed up. He looked at sweep camera film, saw us jinking as we left the target and accused us (very personally, face-to-face with me) of jinking on our runs, thus decreasing our accuracy.

This 44th TFS jet has a single-launch AIM-9B rail and a MER with three M117s hung on the inboard pylon. The outboard pylons could not be jettisoned in flight. On approach to the target pilots often aimed for speeds of up to 540 knots, causing their bombs to bump together on the MERs in the airstream (*D Larsen*)

F-105D 60-0496 with five Mk 83 bombs flies with Snakeye-armed 60-0424 – the aircraft that MiG-killer Maj 'Mo' Seaver was shot down in on a 10 July 1967 *Iron Hand* mission. His rescue report noted that he had 'done a good job of camouflaging himself and was in high grass. This made him very difficult to see. We had asked him to fire a flare, but he became excited and couldn't get his flare loose. It was taped to his pant leg'. Seaver was eventually hauled aboard despite increasing ground-fire, and was 'very muddy and wet'. 60-0496 flew with the Washington, D.C. ANG's 121st TFS post-war (*USAF*)

F-105D 62-4334 *The Bat Bird* was Ed Rasimus' personal aircraft, being known for its ultra reliable Doppler system. MiG-killer 1Lt Karl Richter was flying it on 28 July 1967 as he approached his 200th mission. Hit by AAA on an armed reconnaissance in RP I, he ejected and landed on cruelly sharp karst rocks, sustaining injuries from which he died in the rescue helicopter. Nearing the end of his time with the 34th TFS, Richter had already signed on for a third tour in F-100 Super Sabres. 62-4334 is seen here on 14 November 1965 while serving with the 469th TFS/6234th TFW after being transferred in from the 36th TFS (*USAF*)

'I insisted, in an act that was obviously politically incorrect, that once we rolled in on the target our ass belonged to "Uncle Sam" until we punched the bombs off on target, and that we never wiggled until our bombs were released. Gen Ryan told me not to give him that crap.

'Early in *Rolling Thunder* we had to carry big camera pods on one jet in some flights of four. After several bad incidents where the camera-carrier could not keep up with his squadronmates, thus jeopardising the whole flight, we managed to get that foolishness stopped.'

Very little of the F-105 camera film was of much use for BDA, which relied mainly on film from dedicated reconnaissance aircraft.

July 1967 saw 11 Thunderchiefs destroyed, three of which fell to AAA within the space of four minutes on the 5th when the Takhli wing again bombed railway targets near Kep. Majs Ward Dodge (61-0042) and Dewey Waddell (61-0127) and Capt William Frederick (60-0454) were all captured, although only Waddell returned alive in early 1973.

Three of the nine F-105s destroyed in August were also lost on the same day (the 3rd), although only Capt Wallace Newcomb's 13th TFS jet (58-1154) was shot down. The other two (62-4240 and 61-0139 of the 333rd TFS) collided while refuelling from a KC-135A en route to a target in North Vietnam, Capt William Bischoff being killed.

DOUMER DOWNED

August 1967 also saw the Paul Doumer Bridge finally released from the restricted list. When it became clear that Secretary of Defense McNamara was publicly losing faith in the bombing campaign, and wanted to halt it, the Senate Armed Services Committee forced another 16 targets onto the *Rolling Thunder* list, including the 19-span Paul Doumer Bridge.

One of five rail and road routes identified by the JCS as a main target choice in April 1964, the bridge was the only railway crossing point over the Red River. As such it was the primary route for supplies being brought into Hanoi from Haiphong and China.

The Paul Doumer Bridge was 8437 ft long and 38 ft wide, which in turn meant that the 3000-lb M118 bomb that had been used for other large 'strategic' bridge targets from May 1966 was the weapon of choice.

Target clearance was issued unexpectedly to the 355th TFW on 11 August 1967, and the day's ordnance loads of 750-lb bombs and wing tanks were rapidly replaced by the heavier weapons for an attack that same afternoon. Col John C Giraudo, who had only taken command of the Takhli wing on 2 August, quickly appointed his second-in-command, Col Bob White, as mission leader and 333rd TFS CO Lt Col Bill Norris as mission planner.

Flown by the wing's most experienced pilots, five flights of F-105s from the 355th TFW, a 388th TFW *Wild Weasel* flight and bombers from the 388th and 8th TFWs (as well as three MiGCAP flights from the latter wing)

executed a faultless mission in clear weather. The *Wild Weasels*, led by Lt Col James McInerney (13th TFS CO) and Electronic Warfare Officer (EWO) Capt Fred Shannon, took out two SAM sites immediately and neutralised four more during the course of the mission – both men were subsequently awarded Air Force Crosses for their efforts on the day.

Takhli aircraft penetrated intense AAA, and the second F-105D flight's M118s dropped the middle span of the bridge. Further direct hits were scored by Col Robin Olds' F-4 wave and the 388th TFW F-105s led by 469th TFS CO, Lt Col Harry Schurr. In all, their 94 tons of bombs destroyed one span of the rail link and two road spans. Schurr reported, 'You could see the 3000 "pounders" popping like big orange balls as they struck the bridge'. No jets were lost and an attempted interception by MiGs failed. As usual, the Seventh Air Force ordered a follow-up mission the next day, which was also planned by Lt Col Norris. This too succeeded, and the resulting damage closed the bridge for two months.

In another coincidence of names, Capt Thomas Norris (469th TFS) flew the only F-105D casualty (62-4278) during the 12 August mission. His *Iron Hand* jet was hit by AAA near Gia Lam Airport and he ejected, being captured a short while later.

Although the ingenious North Vietnamese had repaired the bridge by early October, bad weather prevented a re-attack until the 25th of the month, when a force of 21 Takhli F-105s aimed 63 tons of M118s on the bridge. Two spans were dropped for the loss of 354th TFS jet 58-1168 (a MiG killer) – Maj Richard Smith ejected into captivity. A 333rd TFS aircraft (59-1745) was set ablaze by AAA later that same day

SSgt I Reed looked after 62-4326 for the 44th TFS until it was shot down on 17 October 1967 while attacking the Dap Cau railway marshalling yard near Hanoi. Three F-105s were lost from 'Hotrod' flight on that mission, and their pilots were all imprisoned. AAA claimed all three of them either during the roll-in or pull-out for their bomb-runs. Maj Don Odell, in 62-4326, had previously flown the F-86, F-102 and F-106 prior to the Thunderchief (*Don Larsen/ Remington*)

The 469th TFS's 59-1750 *Flying Anvil IV* was painted in the reverse camouflage scheme initially applied to about a quarter of the fleet. The responsibility of SSgt Robert Ames at Korat in 1966, the fighter was the only casualty during the successful attack on the Paul Doumer Bridge on 14 December 1967. With his aircraft hit by AAA as it pulled off the target, Capt James Sehorn (who was on just his seventh combat mission) spent five years as a PoW and eventually retired with the rank of brigadier general in the AFRES (*Don Larsen*)

when Phuc Yen airfield was attacked as part of the ongoing USAF/US Navy suppression of MiG activity, Capt Ramon Horinek being captured.

Further strikes on the bridge caused severe damage on 14 December, when it was the target for 90 3000-lb bombs. Another attack was made four days later, leaving the Paul Doumer Bridge inoperable until the 'bombing halt' began in November 1968. A pontoon bridge was constructed to take part of the railway traffic, however.

HEAVY GREEN

Following the mission hiatus in early 1966 due to persistent bad weather, the USAF looked to the introduction of Project *Combat Skyspot* in June of that year to solve these problems. This system used ground-based MSQ-77 ground radar to allow jets to accurately drop their ordnance on targets in North Vietnam through cloud cover. Although now bombing from above the AAA umbrella, aircraft were still vulnerable to SAMs or MiGs. Indeed, the latter could suddenly appear through the cloud-base, leaving USAF fighter pilots with little time to react.

A paucity of MSQ-77 radars initially confined operations to the lower Route Packages. Six *Skyspot* ground stations were eventually operational by 3 April 1967, and another secret installation was planned under Project *Heavy Green*. A lightweight TSQ-81 bombing radar was airlifted to *Lima Site 85* atop the 5800-ft cliffs of Phou Pha Ti, near the Laotian border and just 110 miles from the key targets around Hanoi. With a clear line-of-sight for radar to cover them all, this location massively enlarged the potential area for radar-controlled bombing in monsoon conditions.

The F-105 units did not work operationally with *Skyspot* until September 1967, when trials were undertaken by the 355th TFW. Their three-war veteran commander at that time, Col John C 'Big Kahuna' Giraudo, personally supervised the flights, which included a mission against the Yen Bai railway marshalling yard. Giraudo was unhappy about the need to fly very close formation with two flights of jets, and with having to keep their IFF switched on – he suspected that the VPAF might use the IFF emissions to guide MiGs onto the Thunderchiefs. Giraudo said that his formation felt like 'the Thunderbirds over Las Vegas', and he therefore requested that the 355th be excused from further participation in radar bombing, fearing greatly increased losses. In his opinion there was no point in the F-105 'playing at being a phoney B-52'. The mission passed to the Korat wing, and their losses did indeed increase.

Lima Site 85 began controlling *Commando Club* missions over Laos in late 1967, and on 18 November, as targets in the Hanoi area were also gradually released, 388th TFW CO Col Edward Burdett led 16 F-105Ds from the 34th and 469th TFSs in a TSQ-81-directed raid on Noi Bai (Phuc Yen) airfield. The latter had been home to MiG-21F-13s of the 921st FR since January 1966.

59-1749 *MARILEE E* (a reverse-camouflaged F-105D) carried the name *Mr Toad* on the opposite flank in 388th TFW service. Tended by SSgt Sailar, it was downed on a *Combat Skyspot* EB-66-led mission on 23 September 1967 near Ban Katoi. The jet's pilot, Maj D S Aunapu of the 469th TFS, was rescued. Mk 82 'lady fingers' low drag general purpose bombs (LDGPs) were favoured by *Iron Hand* flights because they allowed the F-105 to manoeuvre a little better, showed up less obviously in front profile on enemy radar and could be fitted with fuse extenders to cause wide blast destruction at SAM and AAA sites (*Don Larsen via Norm Taylor*)

61-0208 *BLITZKREIG* (also named *Mr Bulldog*) of the 34th TFS was photographed in April 1967. Waiting in Korat's arming area in the blazing sun, and with the heat from up to eight jet effluxes, ensured that all pilots were sweating heavily by the time they took off. 61-0208 was one of nine US aircraft, including three F-105s, lost on 19 November 1967. The Korat wing mounted a large operation against a barge factory at Thuy Phuong, and four jets were downed, including 61-0208. Its pilot, Capt Harrison Klinck of the 469th TFS, was unable to eject before it crashed near Vinh Yen (*Don Larsen*)

THE RED BARON (60-0422) from the 469th TFS/388th TFW was marked up with an experimental tail-symbol to provide the wing's aircraft with some identity amid the anonymity of camouflage. MiG-21 ace Vu Ngoc Dinh was credited with shooting this jet down on 17 December 1967. Some 31 jets from the 388th TFW were intercepted at 16,000 ft by several VPAF fighters as they headed for the Lang Lau railway bridge. 1Lt Jeffrey Ellis ejected ten miles from the target and was captured (*Don Larsen/Remington*)

Two of the four-aircraft *Wild Weasel* anti-radar flight were shot down by top VPAF ace Nguyen Van Coc and his wingman. The first, two-seat F-105F 63-8295, was hit by Van Coc's 'Atoll' missile and both crewmen, Maj Oscar Dardeau and Capt Ed Lehnhoff, were killed. An F-105D (60-0497) in the same flight was also hit by an 'Atoll' and later crashed in Laos – Lt Col William Reed was rescued. The leader of the 'Vegas' strike flight, Maj Leslie J Hauer, was killed when his F-105D (62-4283) took a SAM hit as he prepared to roll in on the target. He ejected but was never heard from again. Finally, Col Burdett's aircraft (62-4221) was crippled by a SAM explosion and he died soon after ejection. The other aircraft jettisoned their bombs when the MiGs appeared. From a 16-aircraft *Club* formation, a quarter had been lost. Three more Thunderchiefs fell to SAMs the following day, including yet another *Wild Weasel* F-105F.

Despite these blows Gen Ryan and Gen William Momyer, head of the Seventh Air Force from July 1966, supported radar bombing, and it continued outside the SAM rings. Towards the end of 1967 the weather was so impenetrable that radar-directed bombing was the only means of striking major targets in the North, and from January through to March 1968, visual bombing was possible on only four days in the Hanoi area.

Lima Site 85 had radar-directed 130 sorties over North Vietnam in November 1967, hitting Yen Bai, Kep, Noi Bai and Hoa Lac, among other vital targets. In December, a further 93 sorties were mounted, and in January, 99 were flown against Yen Bai and storage areas in the North. All involved F-105s, and many more focused on Laotian targets into March, with *Commando Club* strikes on the Tien Cuong railway marshalling yard and, on 10 March, the final strike on the Thai Nguyen

58-1157 *BUBBLES 1* (*Shirley Ann* on the right fuselage) was shot down on 3 January 1968 by MiG-21 ace Nguyen Dang Kinh, who had first evaded an F-4 MiGCAP 25 miles west of Thai Nguyen. Col James Bean, 388th TFW Deputy Operations Officer and a World War 2 P-47 pilot, was taken prisoner. He had flown F-105s since 1960, and helped to develop the aircraft's training manual. Upon returning to Kep, Nguyen Dang Kinh overran the runway on landing, collapsing the fighter's nose gear. The MiG's canopy had to be smashed in order for the ace to be released (*D Larsen*)

Rolling out with six M117s and two QRC-160 pods, 59-1760 was assigned to Korat's 34th TFS. Behind it are revetments full of F-4Es, which replaced the F-105D in the 469th TFS in November 1968, just as *Rolling Thunder* ended. This F-105D, which acquired the nicknames *Lady Jane*, *The Underdog*, *Warlord II* and *Lemon Sucker* while serving with the 388th TFW, flew with the ANG's 121st TFS until April 1977 (*USAF*)

railway hub. Significantly, far more were directed at targets around *Lima Site 85* itself, and on 11 March North Vietnamese sappers overran the site. Because of the extreme secrecy involved in operating the site from a supposedly neutral country, its loss was not admitted by the US government. An accurate assessment of its effectiveness (and of *Rolling Thunder* strikes generally) remains elusive. Indisputably though, for 18 weeks in 1967-68 *Combat Skyspot* was the only way of maintaining sortie rates over North Vietnam.

HEAVY AUTUMN LOSSES

As *Rolling Thunder* continued into the latter part of 1967 the F-105 losses continued, with five in September, a staggering 22 in October (including nine operational losses, several of which were due to the failure of over-stretched J75 engines) 14 in November and three in December.

The 388th had been particularly hard hit during this period, losing 29 jets – seven of them in the space of 72 hours between 18-20 November. Amongst those lost by the wing was vice-commander Col John Flynn (in 62-4231) to a SAM on 27 October and wing commander Col Edward Burdett (in 62-4221), also to a SAM, on 18 November. Finally, on the 3rd of that same month the 388th's Deputy for Operations, World War 2 veteran Col James Bean (in 58-1157), fell victim to a MiG-21.

Following such terrible losses, F-105 wings struggled to maintain an effective mission tempo come the new year. However, with the scaling back of *Rolling Thunder*, the loss rate never again reached the dreadful levels of 1967. Nevertheless, 47 F-105s were lost in 1968.

By then contradictory voices in the USA had confused the Johnson administration's policies. For example, a McNamara-sponsored 'Jason' scientific group had told the President that the bombing had actually increased the North's military capacity, while another advisory group informed him that bombing would force Hanoi to negotiate. The latter view was shared by the British consul general in Hanoi, John Colvin, who witnessed a city where the 'country's endurance had reached its limit' by the end of 1967. However, Vietnamese patience, resolve and faith in their leadership was strong. Haiphong stayed open despite attempts to isolate it by bombing, and F-105 pilots routinely overflew ships, many from America's allies, waiting to unload supplies.

The siege of Khe Sanh and build-up of North Vietnamese troops in the South made the continuation of *Rolling Thunder* inevitable. However, weather restricted bombing

sorties in *Rolling Thunder 57* to just three days per month from January to March 1968, giving the North more time to reinforce its defences.

Robert McNamara stepped down as Secretary for Defense on 1 March 1968, disillusioned and exhausted. His successor, Clark Clifford, advised President Johnson that there was no longer a foreseeable military end to the war, and that the bombing should be reduced to persuade Hanoi to negotiate. As Johnson had also decided to step down, Clifford's proposals were enforced and the 'bomb line' moved south to the 19th parallel. In any case, most of the valuable targets in the North had been destroyed by then, and the air war concentrated once again on supply routes in Laos.

F-105D 61-0194 *THE AVENGER* of the 34th TFS was lost on a truck-strafing run near Dong Hoi on 28 May 1968. Maj Roger Ingvalson, who was the 34th TFS Ops Officer, was taken prisoner. The jet's airbrake petals are in the 'afterburner on' position, apart from the lower segment, which always drooped when hydraulic pressure was run down (*USAF*)

The last *Rolling Thunder* sortie was flown on 1 November 1968, and President Johnson announced the end of the campaign minutes after it had landed. F-105 units continued their missions into Laos, however.

Between 1965 and the end of 1967, 307 F-105s fell from the skies, and out of the total of 397 wartime losses, 274 occurred over the North. In all, 150 pilots were killed and 103 captured. For the North Vietnamese, the cessation of *Rolling Thunder* was merely the end of another chapter in almost a century of defending their independence through tenacity and patience. For them victory meant America abandoning the war. Under its new President, Richard Nixon, a major draw-down of US forces in-theatre began in 1969. The F-105D units were among those to pull out.

With the air war focused on Laos and South Vietnam, the role of the dwindling F-105D force could be transferred to the increasing number of F-4D/Es, with their heavier weapons loads and twin engines for greater survivability. When the 388th TFW commenced its transition to the

F-105D 61-0176 *The Jolly Roger* stands ready in its 357th TFS revetment at Takhli in 1970. Yellow trim extends to its intakes, radar reflector, nose probe and canopy rails, and can also be seen as a band behind the radome (*USAF*)

F-4E in the autumn of 1969, the 44th TFS retained its F-105s and was transferred to Takhli on 15 October. It continued to fly *Wild Weasel* operations from here until the 355th TFW's remaining three units were inactivated on 10 October 1970. Although the F-105Ds had left Southeast Asia, the *Wild Weasel* units continued to provide support for B-52 and RF-4C operations over North Vietnam and Cambodia until October 1974, when the 17th Wild Weasel Squadron (WWS) returned to George AFB. Thus ended ten years of F-105 operations from Thailand.

COLOUR PLATES

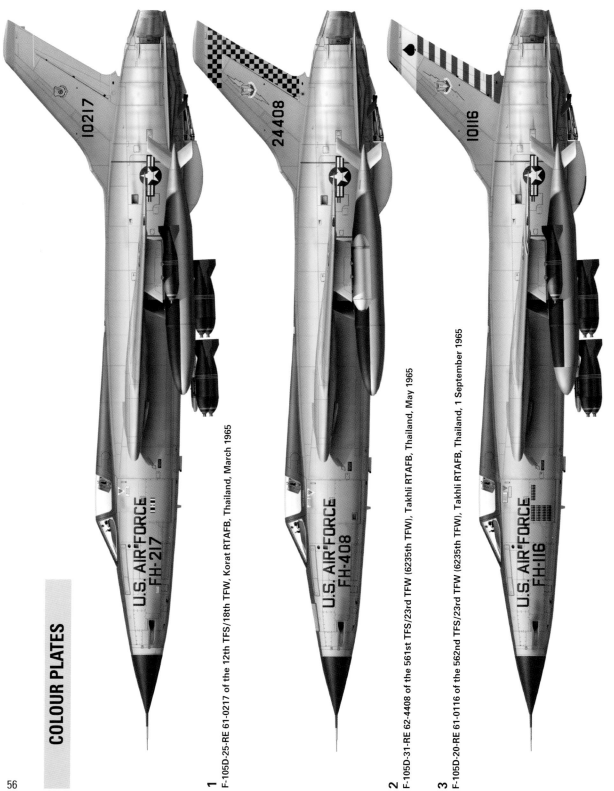

1
F-105D-25-RE 61-0217 of the 12th TFS/18th TFW, Korat RTAFB, Thailand, March 1965

2
F-105D-31-RE 62-4408 of the 561st TFS/23rd TFW (6235th TFW), Takhli RTAFB, Thailand, May 1965

3
F-105D-20-RE 61-0116 of the 562nd TFS/23rd TFW (6235th TFW), Takhli RTAFB, Thailand, 1 September 1965

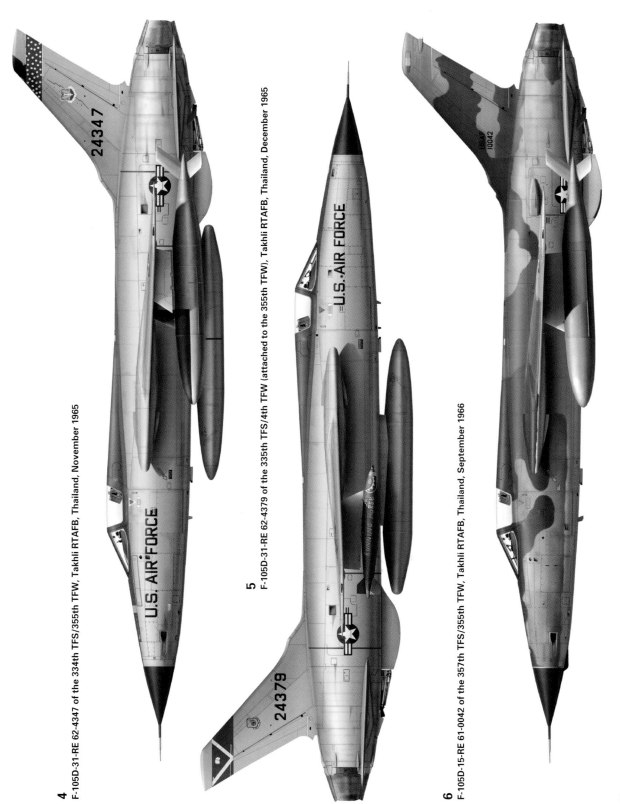

4
F-105D-31-RE 62-4347 of the 334th TFS/355th TFW, Takhli RTAFB, Thailand, November 1965

5
F-105D-31-RE 62-4379 of the 335th TFS/4th TFW (attached to the 355th TFW), Takhli RTAFB, Thailand, December 1965

6
F-105D-15-RE 61-0042 of the 357th TFS/355th TFW, Takhli RTAFB, Thailand, September 1966

57

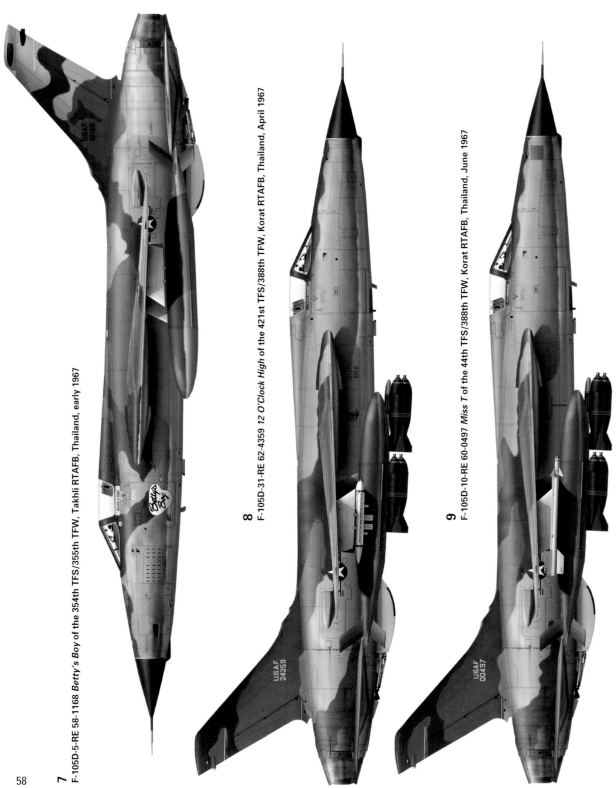

7
F-105D-5-RE 58-1168 *Betty's Boy* of the 354th TFS/355th TFW, Takhli RTAFB, Thailand, early 1967

8
F-105D-31-RE 62-4359 *12 O'Clock High* of the 421st TFS/388th TFW, Korat RTAFB, Thailand, April 1967

9
F-105D-10-RE 60-0497 *Miss T* of the 44th TFS/388th TFW, Korat RTAFB, Thailand, June 1967

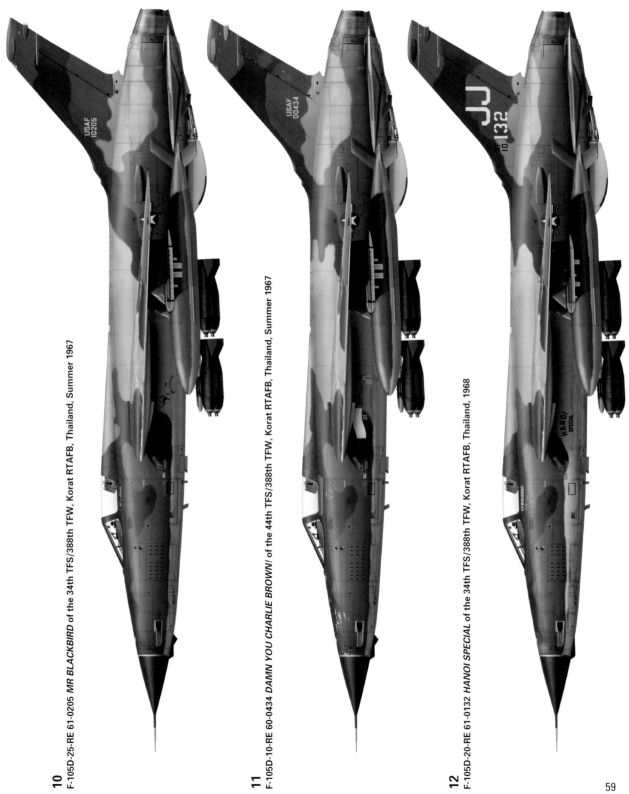

10
F-105D-25-RE 61-0205 *MR BLACKBIRD* of the 34th TFS/388th TFW, Korat RTAFB, Thailand, Summer 1967

11
F-105D-10-RE 60-0434 *DAMN YOU CHARLIE BROWN!* of the 44th TFS/388th TFW, Korat RTAFB, Thailand, Summer 1967

12
F-105D-20-RE 61-0132 *HANOI SPECIAL* of the 34th TFS/388th TFW, Korat RTAFB, Thailand, 1968

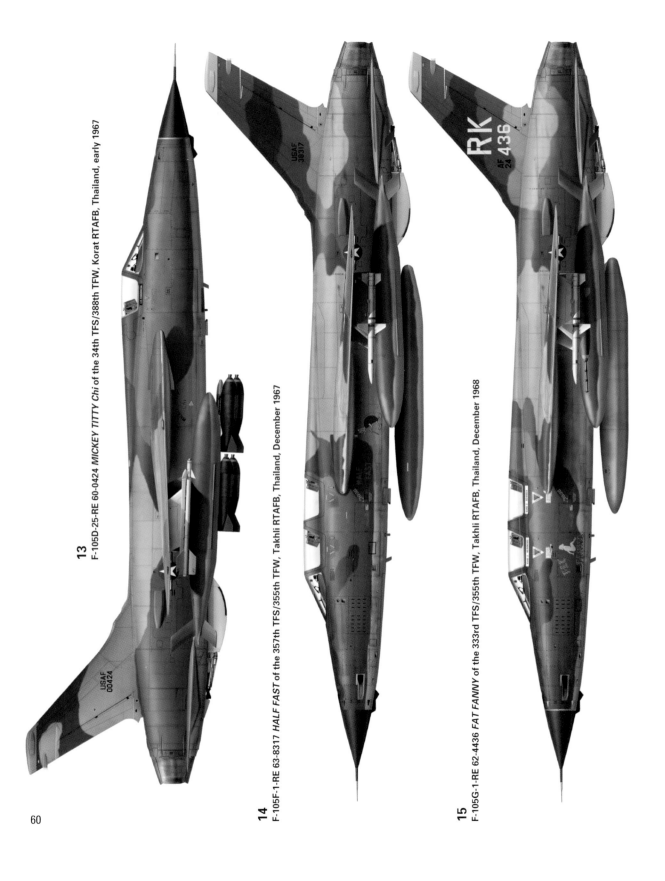

13
F-105D-25-RE 60-0424 *MICKEY TITTY Chi* of the 34th TFS/388th TFW, Korat RTAFB, Thailand, early 1967

14
F-105F-1-RE 63-8317 *HALF FAST* of the 357th TFS/355th TFW, Takhli RTAFB, Thailand, December 1967

15
F-105G-1-RE 62-4436 *FAT FANNY* of the 333rd TFS/355th TFW, Takhli RTAFB, Thailand, December 1968

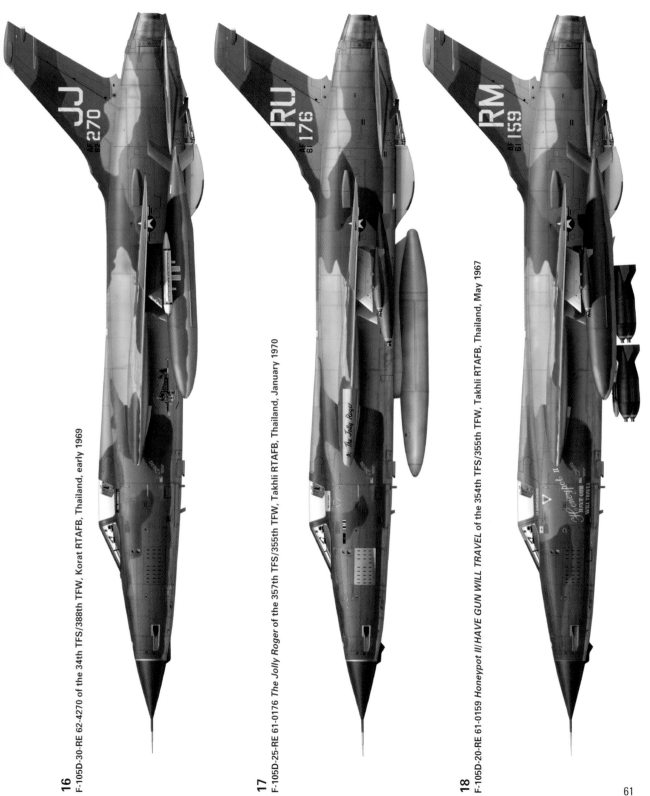

16
F-105D-30-RE 62-4270 of the 34th TFS/388th TFW, Korat RTAFB, Thailand, early 1969

17
F-105D-25-RE 61-0176 *The Jolly Roger* of the 357th TFS/355th TFW, Takhli RTAFB, Thailand, January 1970

18
F-105D-20-RE 61-0159 *Honeypot II/HAVE GUN WILL TRAVEL* of the 354th TFS/355th TFW, Takhli RTAFB, Thailand, May 1967

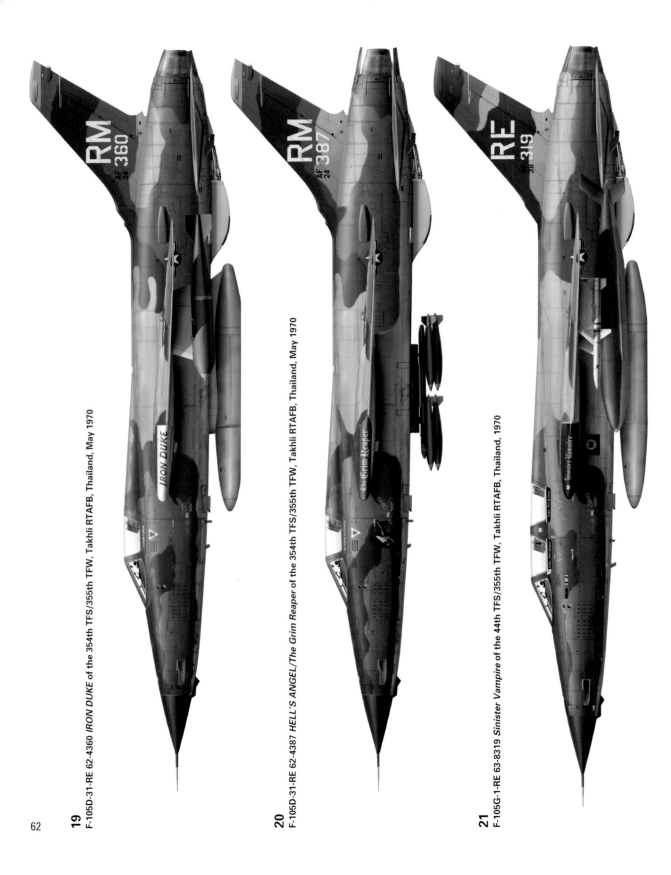

19
F-105D-31-RE 62-4360 *IRON DUKE* of the 354th TFS/355th TFW, Takhli RTAFB, Thailand, May 1970

20
F-105D-31-RE 62-4387 *HELL'S ANGEL/The Grim Reaper* of the 354th TFS/355th TFW, Takhli RTAFB, Thailand, May 1970

21
F-105G-1-RE 63-8319 *Sinister Vampire* of the 44th TFS/355th TFW, Takhli RTAFB, Thailand, 1970

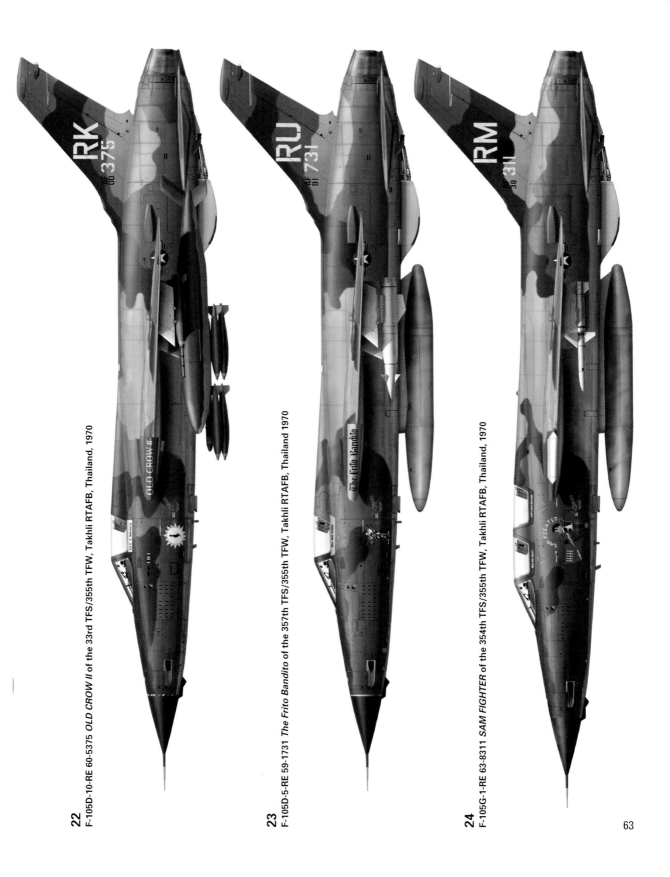

22
F-105D-10-RE 60-5375 *OLD CROW II* of the 33rd TFS/355th TFW, Takhli RTAFB, Thailand, 1970

23
F-105D-5-RE 59-1731 *The Frito Bandito* of the 357th TFS/355th TFW, Takhli RTAFB, Thailand 1970

24
F-105G-1-RE 63-8311 *SAM FIGHTER* of the 354th TFS/355th TFW, Takhli RTAFB, Thailand, 1970

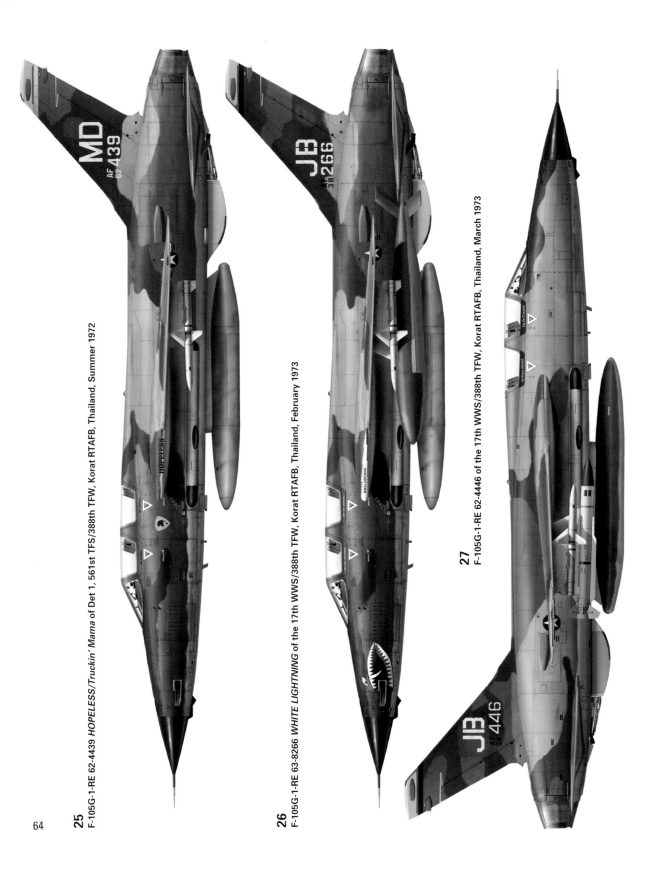

25
F-105G-1-RE 62-4439 *HOPELESS/Truckin' Mama* of Det 1, 561st TFS/388th TFW, Korat RTAFB, Thailand, Summer 1972

26
F-105G-1-RE 63-8266 *WHITE LIGHTNING* of the 17th WWS/388th TFW, Korat RTAFB, Thailand, February 1973

27
F-105G-1-RE 62-4446 of the 17th WWS/388th TFW, Korat RTAFB, Thailand, March 1973

THE MiG KILLERS

Despite flying the majority of their missions as bombers, sometimes in B-17-style straight-and-level formations, F-105 flyers regarded themselves primarily as fighter pilots, flying a formidable jet with gun and missile armament. However, the aircraft's large ordnance-bearing capability, speed and bombing systems predicated its use as a bomber from the inception of Vietnam operations.

The limited MiG threat on early *Rolling Thunder* missions was usually handled by MiGCAP flights of F-100Ds or F-104Cs. As the VPAF gathered strength and introduced the faster, missile-firing MiG-21, the MiGCAP role was passed to F-4C units based at Ubon and Da Nang. While Thunderchief pilots measured success via the number of missions flown and their bombing accuracy, the F-4 crews' reputations depended more on MiG kills. Despite this, in *Rolling Thunder* F-105 pilots encountered MiGs more often than any other US aircrew.

The Thunderchief was not designed for the close-quarters, manoeuvring air-to-air combat that agile MiGs could perform. Even so, crews were credited with 27.5 confirmed MiG-17 kills between 29 June 1966 and 19 December 1967, with credible claims on at least four more. During this period the USAF's designated MiGCAP fighter, the F-4 Phantom II, destroyed 21 MiG-17s, but also downed an equal number of supersonic MiG-21s, using missiles – MiG-21s seldom entered the F-105's gun envelope. Their usual 'one pass, haul ass' tactic meant that they did not stay to fight. In the same period, 70 F-105s were lost, but only 15 to MiGs. The rest fell to the enemy's AAA and SA-2 defences.

A loaded F-105 was more than four times heavier than a MiG-17 but it developed nearly four times as much thrust, giving the jet a top speed at altitude more than double the MiG-17's. It was nearly 30 ft longer too, but only 3 ft wider. Although the MiG-17 had the advantage in dogfights, the F-105 could use superior acceleration and speed to disengage.

Thunderchiefs often carried AIM-9B Sidewinders from December 1966, but the cannon was its principal air-to-air weapon, like the MiG-17. Both aircrafts' guns were effective at distances of up to 3000 ft, although US pilots were advised that the MiG's heavy 37 mm cannon shells were dangerous at up to 5000 ft. Inside gun range, the MiG-17 could use its manoeuvrability to assume an attacking position, with five seconds' firing time to unleash a considerable weight of projectiles (more than 35 lbs per

The 'high drag' dual AIM-9B launcher on a 334th TFS F-105D at Takhli RTAFB. The Sidewinder had a lead-sulphide infrared seeker with a glass dome that abraded easily in flight. The Mk 8 blast-fragmentation warhead weighed ten pounds and the Mk 17 rocket motor gave it a range of about 2.6 miles (*USAF*)

second) from two 23 mm and one slow-firing 37 mm gun, before turning to escape. The F-105's single M61A1 cannon fired up to 89 20 mm rounds (19 lbs in weight) per second. It had twice the firing time of the MiG's armament, but it tended to jam, costing several kill opportunities.

Gun aiming presented problems in both fighters. While the F-105 was an excellent, stable gun-platform, the MiG-17's control limitations and heavy vibration made it much harder to keep on target while firing its guns, and the 34 rounds per second from its three cannon tended to scatter. Forward visibility through the crude ASP-4NM gunsight was further limited by a thick, heavily framed windscreen, although the fighter's bubble canopy gave better all-round visibility than the F-105's, which provided poor rearward vision. The MiG-17 had simple, hardy construction and mechanical control linkages, although the 36-gallon fuel tank situated directly under the tailpipe increased its vulnerability.

In the F-105's cluttered cockpit, the dual-purpose bomb/gunsight was usually set up for bombing, and if MiGs appeared a pilot had to make a complex transition using several fairly inaccessible switches to re-set the sight in air-to-air mode. This process consumed time and attention, often losing the pilot a good firing opportunity. As a result the M61A1 Vulcan gun was triggered as close as possible to the target without the lead-computing gunsight in 100 out of 140 gun attacks, scoring ten kills, once the F-105 had employed its acceleration to close on the MiG in its rearward 'blind' area. The M61A1 emitted a concentrated stream of shells and the target had to be right at the centre of it for a kill. However, a lucky burst, or 'ruddering' the jet to disperse the shots, could saw chunks off a MiG, while a single 37 mm shell hit could fatally damage an F-105.

VPAF fighter pilots were tasked with preventing F-105s from bombing, either by shooting them down or by forcing them to jettison their war-loads so as to turn and defend themselves. Their integrated ground control organisation vectored MiGs into ideal positions for attacking F-105 flights while evading the accompanying MiGCAP

From this homeward-bound 355th TFW formation 62-4242 carried an unofficial MiG kill marking. This aircraft subsequently flew with the 466th TFS post-war. 62-4387 came from the final batch of 135 F-105D-31-REs, and it accumulated 5817 flying hours in its 19 years of USAF service. 61-0161 also survived the Vietnam War, flying with the 457th TFS following its Thunderstick II conversion (*USAF*)

flights. De-conflict with AAA and SAM batteries was usually effectively arranged, and MiG pilots were given exact instructions throughout their interceptions, leaving little room for pilot initiative. Although VPAF tactics varied during *Rolling Thunder*, normally MiG-17s were directed at low and medium altitudes against the heavily laden formations of F-105s during their bomb-runs, while a smaller number of MiG-21s attacked or distracted the MiGCAP flights at higher altitudes or intercepted the high-value *Wild Weasel* F-105s.

All Thunderchief successes were against MiG-17s, which in turn downed seven F-105s. When MiG-21s (first entering the battle on 25 April 1966) increasingly intercepted F-105 formations in coordinated attacks with MiG-17s from December 1966 onwards, 15 Thunderchiefs were destroyed, ten of these in 1967. Although VPAF MiG-21 pilots began claiming F-105s from 7 June 1966 with the loss of Capt J F Bayles' 333rd TFS F-105D (61-0168), all were attributed to AAA by the USAF until 11 July, when Maj W L McClelland had to eject from his 355th TFW F-105D (61-0121) through fuel starvation after a long engagement with the MiG-21s of 921st FR pilots Vu Ngoc Dinh and Dong Van Song. The first F-105D actually shot down by a MiG-21 was possibly 354th TFS CO Lt Col Don Asire's 59-1725 on 8 December 1966, followed by Capt 'Spade' Cooley's 357th TFS jet (60-0502) six days later.

Against the MiG-21, an F-105 had little speed advantage, and the much lighter MiG could accelerate faster. If the Thunderchief pilot tried to use his afterburner he presented the MiG-21 pilot with a better target for his K-13 'Atoll' heat-seeking missiles. A spiralling dive could prevent an 'Atoll' from tracking properly, or an abrupt pull-back on the throttle, together with speed-brake extension, might make the MiG overshoot.

By 1968 MiG tactics had improved, and on 3 January the 388th TFW's veteran deputy for operations Col James Bean was shot down by Nguyen Dang Kinh's MiG-21. Two days later a MiG-17 claimed *Wild Weasel* F-105F 63-8356 from the 357th TFS, and a MiG-21 destroyed Maj Stan Horne's F-105D (60-0489) from the 469th TFS on 14 January.

FIRST SUCCESS

The first F-105 pilot to have a red MiG kill star painted below his cockpit was Maj Fred Tracey, CO of the 421st TFS/388th TFW. He was 'Crab 02' in one of two *Iron Hand* flights that participated in the successful POL attack close to Hanoi on 29 June 1966. The strikers were pursued off the target by three MiG-17s, and when the F-105 flight leader saw them he ordered a diving left turn in afterburner. Tracey's F-105D (58-1156) then took several hits from the MiG's guns, including a 23 mm shell that passed straight through the cockpit, knocking his hand off the throttle and disengaging the afterburner, before exiting through a jagged hole below the windshield.

The F-105's sudden deceleration threw the MiG out in front of Tracey's aircraft, which also had a damaged gunsight. Undeterred, the Thunderchief pilot shot off a short burst of visually aimed 20 mm cannon fire and saw ten hits sparkle on the MiG's left wing-root. The communist jet dived away into clouds at 2000 ft, allowing Tracey to withdraw. 'Crab' leader also fired 200 rounds at the MiG that had attacked his aircraft, but without effect, while 'Crab 04' shot at a fourth MiG-17 'trailer', although

1Lt Karl Richter poses with Maj Fred Tracey's F-105D 58-1156 – the first 'Thud' to score a MiG. It was painted with Richter's name on the canopy for his 100th mission, which was actually flown in his own MiG killer, 59-1766. His flight suit bears the red patch of the 421st TFS (motto 'Ready-Willing-Able') and the coveted '100 Missions F-105' shoulder patch. Richter was killed in action on 28 July 1967 as he approached his 200th mission (*USAF*)

he too missed. On a subsequent mission, Maj Tracey led an F-105 flight 90 miles north of the Chinese buffer zone, allegedly due to a navigational error, but possibly in search of more MiGs.

Korat units scored again on 18 August 1966 when another *Iron Hand* flight sighted two MiG-17s closing on them. Maj Ken T Blank of the 34th TFS quickly manoeuvred his F-105D ('Honda 02', 60-0458, which ended the war with three kills to its credit) behind one of the MiGs and closed to within 500 ft before 'hosing' the target with 200 rounds and seeing it explode as it dived inverted into the ground. Although a second MiG-17 escaped, the VPAF lost 32-year-old Capt Pham Thanh Chung in action that day.

21 September 1966 brought the war's largest engagements to date between the USAF and VPAF when significant numbers of MiGs were launched for the first time. 357th TFS F-105D 62-4371, flown by Capt Glen Ammon, fell to a MiG-21 while attacking the Bac Ninh bridge.

In another bridge attack that same day, 1Lt Karl W Richter was 'Ford 03' in a 388th TFW *Iron Hand* flight (led by an F-105F) for a 40-strong F-105 attack on the Dap Cau bridge. His wingman, Capt Beardsley, noticed MiG-17s approaching the lead *Iron Hand* element, and Richter jettisoned his rocket pods and turned to follow them as they pursued the lead F-105F. He opened fire from 2000 ft at the MiG-17F piloted by Do Huy Hoang (on his first combat mission), which was part of a section led by top MiG-17 ace Nguyen Van Bay. Richter's shells shredded part of the MiG's left wing and it rolled 'wings level'. Hoang lit his VK-1F engine's afterburner, giving Richter the impression that the MiG was on fire.

While Beardsley attempted to hit Van Bay's wingman, Vo Van Man, Richter closed on his target once again, and this time scored hits in the cockpit area, shattering instruments and banging Hoang's head against his large gunsight. Rendered temporarily unconscious, Hoang recovered and grabbed the ejection handle just as more 20 mm rounds sawed into the MiG's wing-root. Van Bay, meanwhile, had evaded the F-105s, and he watched Hoang land safely by parachute. 'His right wing fell off', Richter reported. 'As I flew past I saw the MiG's canopy pop off'.

The 355th TFW's target that day was in the same area, and its jets arrived on the scene just minutes later. Many MiG-17s were still airborne, and the lead F-105 element (call-sign 'Vegas') saw one ahead at low altitude. They dived in pursuit, leaving the second F-105 element to fly high cover. Closing on the target, the flight leader fired a 1.5-second burst that caused some damage, but not enough to prevent the MiG pilot from immediately pulling up in afterburner and turning in behind 'Vegas' flight's lead F-105 to reverse the attack.

Acting as a good wingman, 1Lt Fred A Wilson Jr swung his F-105 (serial unknown) in behind the MiG-17F and without a gunsight fired 280 rounds, cutting pieces from the jet's rear section. He then made a hard left turn and saw the MiG impact the ground. The other pilots pursued a second VPAF fighter, and 'Vegas 03' fired at it, but his gun jammed after only 135 rounds. At that point two MiG-21s appeared and engaged the F-105s, forcing them to dive for the ground, and safety.

The MiGs' GCI had obviously launched more jets than they could control that day, and several of their pilots were left in exposed situations. In addition to the two MiG losses, three were damaged by F-105s that

388th TFW F-105D 60-0518 was credited with a MiG kill for Maj Roy S Dickey on 4 December 1966 (although he may have been flying 62-4278), and it was a 15 July 1969 casualty to ground fire in the Ban Karai Pass. Maj R E Kennedy flew the burning F-105 most of the way back to Korat before ejecting safely (*USAF*)

Maj Roy S Dickey of the 469th TFS scored a MiG-17 kill on only his fourth RP VI mission. The 'bullet-proof' moustache became an essential insurance policy for F-105 pilots. The fate of 1Lt J R Casper, shot down a second time the day after he had shaved his off, was taken as proof of their efficacy – Caspar survived both ejections. Some pilots cultivated extravagant specimens, notably John Piowaty whose well-manicured moustache spanned 12.25 inches! (*USAF*)

had attacked them from unseen positions, and still more could have been hit had three of the F-105s not suffered from jammed guns.

MiG activity in the final three months of 1966 steadily increased. They were encountered by US pilots on all but four days, with more than 85 per cent of the MiG engagements in December involving F-105s and MiG-17s. The two F-105 losses to MiGs that month both fell to MiG-21s. F-105 formations were the MiGs' main objective, although they usually turned away if they saw the jets jettison their bomb-loads. Sometimes they mistook tumbling drop-tanks for bombs. The faster MiG-21s could press home their attacks knowing that the F-105s took time to accelerate after jettisoning ordnance. Alternatively, they tried to catch F-105s as they began their bomb-runs or pulled up from them.

For example, Maj Roy S Dickey of the 469th TFS/388th TFW was climbing away after hitting a railway marshalling yard target on 4 December 1966 when he saw a MiG-17 closing on his element leader, 'Elgin 03'. Four MiGs had followed the strike at lower altitude. Closing to within 700 ft of the MiG-17, Dickey opened fire and soon saw flames blossom from the wing-root to the tail pipe as the jet entered a flat spin at 3500 ft, taking Lt Luu Duc Si to his death. Dickey's F-105D (62-4278) then came under attack from another MiG-17 and he hit the deck, and the afterburner, escaping at a height of just 50 ft.

Inexperience still limited the MiG pilots' success rate. On 14 December a pair of MiG-21s had a perfect intercept established from behind and above an F-105 flight but both pilots fired their 'Atoll' missiles too soon and then missed with follow-up cannon fire.

Operation *Bolo* and other subsequent losses to US fighters significantly reduced VPAF activity in the early months of 1967, but April and May saw their most intensive effort of the war, with 50 engagements being fought with US fighters in April and 72 in May. These clashes meant that by the end of 1967 Takhli's 355th TFW had taken its MiG kill total to 19. March brought three aerial victories, with two by Capt Max C Brestel of the 354th TFS (in 62-4284) on the 10th as the monsoon began to abate. This was the first time that a US pilot had claimed a double kill, and they came during a flak suppression operation by 'Kangaroo' flight near the Thai Nguyen steel mill. This proved to be a momentous raid, for it included Capt Merlyn Dethlefsen's Medal of Honor SAM site attack and MiG-defeating RESCAP for a downed F-105F crew.

Prior to claiming his kills, Capt Brestel ('Kangaroo 03') had already distracted two MiG-21s that were lining up on his flight leader, Lt Col Philip Gast, by turning towards them, before continuing with his bomb run. Four MiG-17s then made for the F-105s as they pulled off the target. Max Brestel, famous for his powerful eyesight, reported;

'I observed all MiGs light their afterburners. Col Gast began firing at one of the first two MiGs. I observed the second two begin firing at Col Gast. I called a break and closed to within 300-500 ft of the No 4 MiG. I fired an approximate 2.5-second burst at him as he was in a right turn. I observed hits in the left wing, fuselage and canopy and a fire in the left wing root. I did not see the pilot bail out, and doubt if he was alive since hits were observed in the cockpit and the canopy broke up. The aircraft rolled over and hit the ground under my left wing, watched also by "Kangaroo 04", 1Lt Bob Weskamp.

'I then closed to within 300 ft of the No 3 MiG, which was firing at Col Gast. He was in a right turn and again I fired a 2.5-second burst, observing hits in the wing, fuselage, etc. He also reversed to the left and I fired another 2.5-second burst, observing more hits and pieces flying off the jet. It appeared to flip back over my canopy and disappeared behind me in a violent pitch-up or tumble. The MiG was totally out of control.'

Col Robert Scott, CO of the 355th TFW, scored the third F-105 kill of the month when, on 26 March, he claimed a MiG-17 in the 333rd TFS's 59-1772. Attacking a target near Hoa Lac airfield, he took his 'Leech' flight close enough to the runway to see a MiG-17 taking off as they pulled up from a bomb run. Airfield attacks were not yet permitted, and MiGs could only be engaged if they presented a direct airborne threat. Col Scott was ready for that;

'I began a left turn to approximately 150 degrees to follow the MiG for possible engagement. At this time I observed three more MiG-17s orbiting the airfield at about 3000 ft in single-ship trail with 3000-5000 ft spacing. I then concentrated on the nearest MiG-17 and pressed home my attack. As I closed, the jet began to turn to the right. I followed the MiG, turning inside and opening fire. I observed ordnance impacting on the left wing and pieces of material tearing off. At this time the MiG began a hard left descending turn. I began an overshoot and pulled off high and to the right. The last time I saw the MiG it was extremely low at approximately 500 ft, rolling nose-down.'

The VPAF lost Lt Vu Huy Luong in that combat – its 37th acknowledged pilot casualty.

19 April 1967 was an outstanding day for the 355th TFW, with four MiG-17s destroyed, a fifth damaged and a Medal of Honor awarded to 357th TFS pilot Maj Leo K Thorsness. An F-105F (63-8341) from Thorsness' 'Kingfish' *Wild Weasel* flight was shot down, however. 'Kingfish' had been intercepted by up to ten MiG-17s as it approached

F-105D 62-4284, seen here with a 67th TFS bridge-buster flight in October 1965 and armed with a pair of AGM-12B Bullpups, eventually displayed three MiG kill markings – two for Capt Max Brestel on 10 March 1967 and one for Capt Gene Basel on 27 October 1967. Lead aircraft 62-4328 joined the 466th TFS post-war, and 62-4231 (foreground, with M117s) was one of three F-105Ds shot down the same day as Basel's MiG kill. Strike leader Col John Flynn, 388th TFW Deputy Commander and a fighter pilot since 1942, was hit by an SA-2 as he dived on the Canal des Rapides Bridge. After his release from imprisonment in 1973, Flynn eventually became Inspector General of the USAF (*USAF*)

the target – SAM sites near Xuan Mai. 'Kingfish 03' and '04', sent to the northern sector of the target area, each entered separate dog-fights with MiGs, while Thorsness and his EWO, Capt Harry Johnson, pressed on to fire their Shrikes at active SAM sites further south. It was the start of a 50-minute fight for 'Kingfish 01', who then heard from 'Kingfish 02' that their F-105F was showing an overheat light, probably from AAA damage. Majs Thomas Madison and Thomas Sterling ejected, and Thorsness began RESCAP for them.

Meanwhile, 'Kingfish 03' and '04' emerged from their MiG encounters with damage (one had

Maj Leo K Thorsness and Capt Harry Johnson pose for the camera with their F-105F at Takhli RTAFB in early 1967 – about halfway through their tour. When their jet was hit by an 'Atoll' missile on 30 April 1967, they 'punched out' at well above the 525 knots 'safe' ejection speed. The blast of air ripped off Thorsness' helmet, forced his lower legs outwards at 90 degrees, causing terrible injuries and tore away a quarter of the panels in his parachute canopy (*USAF*)

an inoperative afterburner) that forced them to head for home, leaving Thorsness and Johnson in the sole aircraft over the target, protectively circling 'Kingfish 02's' crew as they parachuted down. 'Kingfish 02' Johnson spotted a MiG-17 heading eastwards at their 'nine o'clock' position and Thorsness made a series of S-turns to get behind it, soon positioning his F-105F (63-8301) in the MiG's 'six o'clock';

'I initially opened fire (300 rounds) from an estimated 2000-1500 ft in a right hand shallow pursuit curve. No impacts were observed. Within a few seconds we were in the "six o'clock" position, with 75-100 knots of overtake speed. I fired another burst of 300 rounds, then pulled up to avoid both the debris and the MiG. It was approximately 100 ft low and to our left. The two red stars were clearly discernible, one on top of each wing, and several rips were noted on the battered left wing. Prior to the MiG impacting the ground Capt Johnson sighted a MiG-17 at our "6.30 position" approximately 2000 ft back. I pulled into a tighter turn, selected afterburner and lowered the nose. I again looked at the crippled MiG and saw it impact the ground in what appeared to be a rice field.'

Maj Thorsness then went to find a tanker, returning to the battle area to continue his RESCAP effort. He had only 500 rounds left, but a helicopter and two A-1E 'Sandy' escorts had by then arrived to retrieve Madison and Sterling – both men were captured, however.

Thorsness knew there were still at least five MiGs threatening the recovery, and he attacked three of them as he charged back into the fray. One was seriously damaged (a probable second kill), but Thorsness ran out of ammunition before he could finish it off. He remained in the rescue area, however, hoping to draw away further MiGs. Four more duly appeared, and Thorsness eluded them in a wild chase in afterburner through winding mountain passes. When the MiGs broke off their pursuit and headed back in the direction of the 'Sandy' rescuers, Thorsness returned once more, advising the A-1 pilots to 'keep turning'.

Another F-105 arrived to relieve 'Kingfish 01's' one-man war, and he urgently went in search of a tanker again. As Thorsness made contact with one, he heard another F-105 pilot radio that he was down to 800 lbs of fuel – sufficient for a few minutes' flight-time. Thorsness directed 'his' tanker north to rescue the other pilot, who was able to link up with the KC-135 just seconds before his engine flamed out. With his engine throttled back, Thorsness coaxed his F-105F 70 miles to Udorn RTAFB, landing with 'Empty' on the fuel gauges.

'Nitro' flight of the 354th TFS had arrived over Xuan Mai just minutes after 'Kingfish', and its pilots engaged 11 more MiG-17s. Flight leader Maj Jack Hunt (in 58-1168) set up his AIM-9B. From December 1966, element-lead F-105s (the 'shooters' in the standard USAF 'fluid four' combat formation, with flight members Nos 2 and 4 protecting the 'shooters') usually carried an AIM-9B. As the MiG threat increased Sidewinder carriage became more general. Col Broughton recollected;

'We were always short of Sidewinders, thus the number carried depended on how many we had at engine start time. If we had them, we loaded them. They were always nice to have along in case you got on a MiG and had time to set the switches up to get the missile ready to fire. The multiple switch actions required to go from bombs to Sidewinders was ridiculously complex, and far too time and attention consuming to be combat-acceptable. The switches were tough to find and activate.'

A shortage of F-4 Phantom II MiGCAPs was sometimes alleviated by tasking the first F-105 flight as an extra MiGCAP flight, with gunsights set for air-to-air, once it had completed its bombing run. F-4Cs without ECM pods had been unable to follow the F-105s into the SA-2 'rings' after SAM operators started hitting them, rather than the pod-protected fighter-bombers. This opened the way in late 1966 for more MiG attacks on the F-105 formations near to their targets. F-4s at last began to receive QRC-160-8 (AN/ALQ-87) pods in early 1967.

Returning to the action on 19 April, Maj Hunt's missile failed to find his target, as did his gun in an attack on a second MiG-17. There were plenty of targets, however, and when he fired on a third MiG-17 using his gunsight, Hunt 'observed numerous hits and flashes coming from the top of the fuselage just behind the canopy'. The VPAF fighter made a hard diving turn to the right and its demise was later confirmed.

In 'Nitro 03' position, Maj Fred Tolman closed to gun-firing range on another MiG-17. 'I fired approximately 300 rounds of 20 mm at him and observed hits around his canopy section. The MiG passed by my aircraft (F-105D 62-4384) going to my "six o'clock" position. I engaged afterburner and performed a high-climbing turn for re-engagement. Upon sighting the MiG again I noted a trail of white smoke coming from his tailpipe. I saw him roll slowly to the left and start a gentle descent'. The kill was confirmed through gun-camera film.

'Panda' flight was next on the scene, led by Capt William E Eskew in F-105D 62-4364. He and his wingman, Capt Paul Seymour, fired at some MiG-17s, causing damage, but the flight was then diverted to the failing RESCAP effort for 'Kingfish 02' over Suoi Rut. Eskew was told that a 'Sandy' pilot was being fired on by the four MiG-17s that Leo Thorsness had earlier distracted. Minutes earlier, VPAF pilots, Tan, Tho and Trung, had killed 'Sandy' leader Maj John Hamilton.

'Panda' flight blasted straight through the circling MiGs at Mach 1.1, allowing the 'Sandy' driver to escape. The lead MiG broke away too, and

Eskew followed, firing an AIM-9B at him. It passed 15 ft from the MiG without detonating. 'Panda 03', Capt Howard Bodenhamer, also fired at a MiG-17 and Eskew saw an explosion which convinced him that the MiG was destroyed – the kill was not confirmed, however. Eskew's wingman, Capt Paul Seymour, fired on a fourth MiG that had turned behind Eskew. 'Panda 04' (Capt Robert Hammerle), meanwhile, pulled in behind a MiG that was gaining a firing solution on Bodenhamer's jet.

This circular fight (a variation on the MiGs' 'wagon wheel' tactic at that time) at an altitude of 3000 ft ended when Seymour's gunfire forced the MiG off Eskew's tail and possibly shot it down, allowing Eskew two bursts at his own target, which in turn ran for Hanoi. At a range of 1000 ft he placed his gunsight 'pipper' on the MiG's canopy and saw 50-75 hits on the upper fuselage, some of which must have found the main fuel tank. 'As I pulled up to avoid a collision with the MiG, he exploded directly beneath my aircraft. I saw the red fireball and was shaken by the shock. I saw the wreckage of his aircraft burning on the ground'. For a moment Seymour thought he had rammed the MiG. He then turned back to assist Bodenhamer, who still had two MiGs to contend with, and drew one away. Bodenhamer turned his F-105 after the latter jet and fired his missile without result as 'Panda' flight departed in urgent need of fuel.

28 April brought two more MiG-17 kills for Takhli's total in attacks on the Han Phong causeway, near Hanoi. 'Spitfire' flight leader Maj Harry Higgins was flying F-105D 59-1772 (Col Scott's MiG killer) on this occasion. As his flight pulled up from its bomb-run, they were 'mobbed' by nine MiG-17s. Maj Higgins sighted a MiG at his 'two o'clock' and began a turning fight in which he hauled his F-105 into the jet's rear quarter while simultaneously performing the complex AIM-9 switch set-up. He fired the missile at 1000 ft but the MiG pilot tightened his turn and the Sidewinder could not follow it, missing by 1000 ft.

Higgins rejoined with his wingman, 1Lt Gordon Jenkins, and as they egressed the target area they spotted two more MiG-17s approaching them from almost head-on, firing their cannon at them. Higgins and Jenkins returned the fire with short, ineffective bursts, and then went in pursuit of the two MiGs, which had a considerable lead on the F-105s by the time the American jets had completed their turns. Breaking off the chase, the two 357th TFS pilots once again turned for home, but yet another MiG appeared and Higgins lit his afterburner for a third duel. Setting his armament switches for 'guns', Higgins cut across inside the MiG pilot's fairly shallow turn, firing from 1500 ft;

'As I prolonged the firing I noticed that the MiG began to smoke and flames erupted from his left wing root. He began a steep descending turn with the left wing down at approximately 1000 ft.'

Higgins then had to break off as two more MiG-17s had latched onto his tail and were firing at him from 1000 ft. He 'unloaded' his fighter in a steep dive and sped to safety, seeing the stricken MiG 'burning and spiralling towards the ground at less than 500 ft'. Like other fighter pilots at that time, Higgins must have felt that more reliable weapons could, in his case, have given him three kills that day rather than one.

Lt Col Arthur Dennis led 'Atlanta' flight (in F-105D 60-0504) over the same target six minutes later, and once again the MiG-17s tried to ambush them as they completed their bomb runs. Closing on one of the

VPAF fighters, Lt Col Dennis got a good acquisition tone in his headset, but when he fired the AIM-9B it failed to guide properly. Switching to 'guns', he fired initially from a range in excess of 3000 ft;

'I was still too far out for a good firing pass. I continued closing to 1500 ft and began firing, closing to 700 ft when the MiG burst into a large ball of flame. It continued to burn and trail smoke as it went into a steeper turn to the right and nosed over into a wide spiral towards the ground.'

Two days after this epic battle Capt Thomas C Lesan was leading his 'Rattler' flight to their Bac Giang railway marshalling yard target in F-105D 60-0498 when they were attacked twice by three MiG-17s 'prior to pop (climb to begin the attack dive) and again at the top of the pop prior to the bomb run. I continued my bomb run', Lesan reported, 'and jinked constantly right after delivery. At this moment I sighted two MiG-17s at my "11 o'clock" position 3000 ft high and 3000 ft out. I jettisoned my 450-gallon drop tanks, and with my afterburner still engaged from the bomb-run, began to pursue the two MiGs.

'As I started to track the No 2 MiG they both started a rolling, descending turn, and I followed. I tracked and opened fire at 1000 ft. I fired 100 rounds, noting hits impacting down the left side of the forward fuselage and the left wing. With such a great rate of closure I had to break left to avoid collision with the MiG. I rolled right and observed the jet slowly levelling out with its left wing in flames'. Maj James Middleton, following a mile behind Lesan, saw the MiG spin out of control.

Sadly, Thorsness and Johnson were shot down that same day by MiG-21 pilot Le Trong Huyen just 72 hours away from completing their tour. They spent the next six years in appalling prison conditions. Upon his release Maj Thorsness was awarded the Medal of Honor in October 1973 and Johnson later received the Air Force Cross.

30 April also marked the loss of two 355th TFW F-105Ds to MiG-21s, with Capt Joseph Abbott falling to ace Nguyen Van Coc and 1Lt Robert Abbott to his wingman, Nguyen Ngoc Du. The success enjoyed by the MiG-21 on this day was a graphic reminder of the very different challenge it presented to the F-105 compared with the MiG-17.

The 'May Massacre' of 1967, in which USAF fighters destroyed 26 MiGs in 72 aerial battles for the loss of just two F-4Cs severely damaged the VPAF. It also partly offset the ongoing attrition to AAA, which cost ten F-105s that month. Effective anti-fighter tactics also meant that only 15 strike aircraft had to jettison their ordnance in order to combat MiGs.

Five VPAF jets were downed by the 355th TFW and one by a Korat-based pilot in May. Capt Jacques Suzanne of the 333rd TFS was the first to taste success when he led 'Crossbow' flight into combat on the 12th. Five MiG-17s attempted to engage the leading 'Warhawk' F-105 strike flight, prompting Suzanne to turn into them. He opened fire at 4000 ft and again at 800 ft and the MiG began to trail white smoke and fell away. 'Crossbow 02', Capt Lawrence Cobb, saw it strike the ground in a bright flash. Suzanne's jet (61-0159) would ultimately complete 6094 flying hours by June 1981 – 2000 hours more than Republic had intended.

The biggest aerial battles up to that point in the war took place between 12-14 May. Seven MiGs were downed on the 13th (five by F-105 pilots) without the USAF suffering any losses in return. Sidewinders were used successfully by F-105s for the first time for two of these kills.

Lt Col Philip Gast was leading the first 354th TFS flight (in F-105D 60-0501), re-attacking the Yen Vien railway marshalling yard, when MiG-17s patrolling at 1000 ft attempted to intercept the fighter-bombers as they came off the target. He turned his flight to the rear of the MiGs, and the latter then reversed to initiate a head-on attack. Gast fired an AIM-9B at the MiGs' leader at a distance of about 5000 ft, but the missile ran out of thrust and fell short. Capt Charles Couch, leading the other element, also got a good tone on his missile, but he judged that it had locked onto the sun – a familiar problem with heat-seeking missiles.

Gast resorted to his gun at 3000 yards, firing repeatedly at the lead MiG until it passed them. His wingman, Maj Alonzo Ferguson, looked back and saw the MiG in flames. Couch, firing at his opposite number in the MiG-17 flight, pressed home his attack until the last moment, when the VPAF pilot made a hard left break. It took 'violent evasive action to avoid a head-on collision, and the MiG could very likely have entered a spin'.

A pilot in the following F-105 flight saw a MiG pilot eject and another communist jet in a tight spin. That flight was led by Maj Robert Rilling (in 60-0522), and the two 'wheels' of MiGs, one at high altitude and another one lower down, were still in the Yen Vien area as the jets departed from their target. Seeing them, Rilling's 'Random' flight lit afterburners and headed for the closest two MiG-17s. The flight lead launched his AIM-9B and saw it detonate under the tail of a MiG, the missile's fragmentation warhead cutting into the fighter's rear fuselage and starting a fire. 'I followed the jet through a 180-degree left turn in an attempt to use the Vulcan cannon. After completing that manoeuvre the MiG rolled hard right and down and impacted the ground'.

'Random 03' was Maj Carl D Osborne (in 62-4262), and he chased another MiG-17 until he finally selected an AIM-9B shot;

'I rolled into a slight right bank and the tone on the AIM-9 peaked up normally. Only a ten-degree left bank was required to hold the gunsight reticule on the MiG. The tone was holding good so I fired the missile, and it began tracking and detonated at the MiG's "3-4 o'clock" position. He

F-105D 60-0522 was photographed serving with the 357th TFS during a 1968 mission. One of the two MiG kill stars painted ahead of its ejection triangle was scored by Maj Robert Rilling with an AIM-9B on 13 May 1967 in a massive aerial engagement that saw five F-105 pilots each claim a MiG-17 destroyed. Details for the second star remain unknown. 60-0522 was downed by AAA on 14 September 1968, its pilot, Capt D M Tribble, being rescued after ejecting over Laos (*USAF*)

immediately turned left and began trailing smoke. My lead (Rilling) called that he had also scored a hit on the other MiG, and to go after them. I made a hard left turn and saw the MiG I had fired at still trailing smoke and descending.'

The day's seventh MiG-17 fell to Maj Maurice 'Mo' Seaver, flying as 'Kimona 02' of the 13th TFS. Once again MiGs appeared as he pulled away from his bomb run, and he aimed for a camouflaged jet about 1000 ft ahead of him. Apparently the VPAF pilot did not see him, and the 20 mm shells from Seaver's F-105D (60-0497) took the wing off the enemy fighter, sending it spinning away to the right.

The heavy losses of MiGs and pilots in May (four on 19 May alone, including Nguyen Van Coc's wingman, Vo Van Man) were perhaps partly due to inexperience, or simply to the strain on a small force that was flying up to 78 sorties a day. Certainly, the aggressive, well calculated tactics and effective gunnery of the F-105 squadrons was a major factor.

June 1967 brought two more kills, the first falling to Maj Ralph Kuster of the 13th TFS (in 60-0424) on the 3rd. Six miles from the target he saw three MiG-17s orbiting at 500 ft ahead of his flight, so he turned towards them. 'Hambone' flight entered the MiGs' defensive 'wheel' for almost two revolutions before Capt Larry D Wiggins (in 61-0069) launched his AIM-9B at the third MiG-17. It detonated beside the fighter's tailpipe, after which it emitted dense white smoke. Wiggins followed up with 376 rounds from his M61A1, and the MiG exploded when it hit the ground.

Moments earlier Maj Kuster, who was tracking two MiG-17s ahead of his element, was given priority by 'Hambone 01' to attack one from his advantageous position. Kuster's target was in a typically tight left turn, forcing him to fire a burst with 6g on his aircraft at a 45-degree angle off. He had begun a 'yo-yo' manoeuvre to reduce his overshoot when the MiG suddenly reversed his turn to the right. Kuster continued firing short bursts at the elusive fighter as it dived in a smooth left turn that put the F-105 pilot in danger of overshooting, even though he was pulling maximum 'g'. He jerked the F-105's control column back repeatedly, and this eventually gave him enough lead angle on the target.

Firing from a distance of just 200 ft, Kuster saw the MiG-17 pass through his stream of 20 mm shells. Its left wing exploded near a

Maj 'Moe' Seaver's MiG killer 60-0497 *MISS T* is seen here with twin Sidewinders, although its shoot-down was one of the majority that used the gun. Lacking an effective air-to-air radar like that fitted to the F-4 Phantom II, F-105 pilots relied on good eyes to detect MiG threats, since warnings from other sources were not always timely. 60-0497 was shot down by a 921st FR MiG-21 on 18 November 1967, its pilot, Lt Col William Reed of the 469th TFS, successfully ejecting and being rescued (*Don Larsen via Norm Taylor*)

This Korat flightline view includes F-105D 60-0424 (second from left) in reverse camouflage, nicknamed *MICKEY TITTY Chi* and flown by Maj Ralph Kuster as 'Hambone 02' when he shot down a MiG-17 on 3 June 1967. No ejection was seen before the MiG crashed, and the VPAF recorded the death of Lt Pham Tan Duan during that day's combat (*USAF*)

Frames from Ralph Kuster's gun-camera film on 3 June 1967. Lt Phan Tan Duan was recorded as a VPAF loss that day (*USAF*)

44th TFS F-105D (60-0445) was originally identified as being Ralph Kuster's MiG killer, although it was later established that he achieved his victory in 60-0424. This jet was, however, the first F-105 to land in Europe when it was delivered to the 36th TFW at Bitburg AB on 13 May 1961. The pilot on that occasion was 1Lt Gary Retterbush, who subsequently claimed a MiG-21 kill on 12 September 1972 in an F-4E from the 35th TFS/388th TFW (*Don Larsen via Norm Taylor*)

drop-tank and the F-105 was suddenly surrounded by smoke and debris as he passed only 25 ft below the flaming wreck. Seconds later the MiG crashed inverted.

Wiggins's F-105D, provocatively decorated as *Cherry Girl*, spent a year in combat with the 388th TFW. 'Moe' Seaver, Wiggins and James Kasler had been members of the five-man USAFE F-105D team at the June 1965 NATO competition at Chaumont, in France. The other two were Capt Dave Duart, downed in an F-105F on a February 1967 *Iron Hand*, and Maj Ray Kingston, who became the 'high-time' F-105 pilot. Kasler narrowly missed a MiG kill on 19 July 1966, despite being involved in the longest MiG battle of the war up to that time.

1Lt David Waldrop III's F-105D *Hanoi Special* (61-0132) flew in a Yen Vien railway marshalling yard mission on 23 August. Once again, the MiG-17s followed the bombing run after two 555th TFS F-4Ds in the MiGCAP led by Col Robin Olds had been downed by Nguyen Van Coc's MiG-21 flight and two others by AAA. MiGs were more numerous at this time as SAMs had been partially neutralised by ECM pods.

From the nine F-105 flights committed to the mission, Maj Elmo C Baker's 59-1752 fell victim to AAA, although MiG pilot Cao Thanh Tinh claimed it. As Waldrop pulled off his target with a 6.5g climb, he saw another F-105 ahead of him flying straight and level at 400 knots with a pair of MiG-17s closing on it, firing their guns. He instantly

jettisoned his wing-tanks and bomb rack, engaged afterburner and came in below and behind the MiGs. Waldrop's gunsight failed at this point, so an AIM-9B was his best hope – except that he could not be sure it was not 'growling' at the F-105 being chased, rather than the MiG. Instead, he chose to fire blind at the VPAF fighter with his cannon.

Waldrop had built up 350 knots of overtake speed by now, and he powered past the MiG after firing at it, spread his airbrakes and rolled inverted. Through the clouds he saw a second MiG-17 in afterburner, so he rolled level and aimed visually again, scoring hits all over the cockpit area. 'Shortly afterwards fire shot out from his wingtips and midway across the wing, and he started a slow roll over to the right. He continued rolling right on in and blew up when he hit the ground', Waldrop recalled post-mission. Robin Olds witnessed the fighter's demise too;

'The MiG was diving towards the ground with flames coming out of its tailpipe. The jet wasn't in afterburner. It was on fire. There was that great, great, huge "Thud" right behind him with fire coming out of his nose. It was like a shark chasing a minnow.'

Nobody saw the pilot, probably Lt Le Van Phong, eject.

'Crossbow 01', Maj Billy Givens, also pursued a MiG that was chasing an F-105D, and he fired 900+ rounds at it, causing damage that prompted him to lodge a 'probable' kill claim. This was later denied, as was a second claim made by Waldrop for the first MiG that he had attacked. Col Olds had phoned to confirm his first, and in his opinion Waldrop had downed two MiGs. Although this was supported by the 388th TFW, analysis of the evidence resulted in only one award.

There was little MiG activity until October, when a renewed VPAF effort finally brought permission for strikes on Phuc Yen airfield. During a bridge attack at Dai Loi on the 18th, three of the four F-105 strike flights tangled with MiGs. 'Wildcat 04', Maj Donald M Russell of the 333rd TFS, was last off the target, and a MiG-17 crossed his path as he climbed in afterburner to rejoin his flight. Russell (in 62-4394) cut his speed as he followed the fighter, which was clearly planning to attack another 'Wildcat' Thunderchief. He quickly attained a good position and fired from 1000 ft, Russell reporting, 'I noticed flames from both sides aft of the cockpit area. I followed him for a few moments and saw the fire increase. The aircraft rolled right and headed straight down in flames'.

Capt Gene Basel of the 354th TFS was piloting 62-4384 as 'Bison 02' on 27 October. Already credited with Capt Max Brestel's two kills, this jet scored the final F-105D MiG victory of the war. Basel and his element leader joined the flak suppressors after their second element had aborted, and they flew into a maelstrom of SAMs and 85 mm AAA near their Hanoi target that claimed the vice-commander of the 388th TFW, Col John Flynn (in 62-4231).

As they left the target area, Basel sighted two MiG-17s ahead – the first he had ever seen – moving in behind another F-105 flight. Basel approached unseen and opened fire at 2000 yards. His target, a green-camouflaged MiG, turned abruptly, streaming fire, and 1Lt Cal Tax in the following flight saw it jettison its tanks and dive away in flames. Basel's kill was confirmed by his 16 mm gun-camera evidence. Basel was subsequently forced to eject from 62-4385 after it was hit by AAA during a POL attack in Laos on 28 February 1968. He was recovered.

F-105G 63-8329 in its 333rd TFS days, crewed by Maj Wallace and Capt Hoynacki in January 1970, has an AGM-45 outboard and an AGM-78 Standard ARM on the inboard pylon. *Cooter* carried two MiG kills from 1967 marked up beneath its cockpit at this time. The first was claimed by Maj George Guss, who hit the 'master panic button', jettisoning all his ordnance and bomb racks into the path of a pursuing MiG-17. On 19 December 1967 Maj Robert Huntley also claimed a MiG-17 with 20 mm gunfire during an *Iron Hand* attack on Phuc Yen airfield. Both claims were disallowed, however, whilst a third MiG kill star that appeared erroneously on 63-8320 was probably the shared victory scored by Majs William Dalton and James Graham in this very aeroplane on 19 December 1967 (*USAF*)

Two F-105F crews from the same 355th TFW *Iron Hand* flight made the final Thunderchief MiG kills, although one was shared with F-4D crew Majs Joseph Moore and George McKinney of the 435th TFS/8th TFW on 19 December, as McKinney explained;

'Our CAP flight and another F-4 formation were joining up with F-105s when the "Thuds" were jumped by a large number of MiG-17s. To put it mildly, a giant "furball" ensued. Maj Moore spotted a MiG-17 three miles ahead at our "12 o'clock" and I obtained a radar lock-on. As we were closing to maximum Sparrow range an F-105 with a MiG-17 in hot pursuit flew directly across our flight path. Immediately forsaking what appeared to be a sure kill, Joe Moore turned hard right to help the "Thud" with his little MiG problem.'

Their F-4D was carrying a gun pod, and they fired at the MiG from 1500 yards, seeing strikes on its rear fuselage and white smoke. McKinney continued, 'At about 2130 hrs that evening we received a call from Seventh Air Force saying that there were conflicting claims for the MiG kill, and we and an F-105F crew would be awarded a half-share in the victory. That's how I became the only "half ace" of the Vietnam War!'

The F-105F crew in question consisted of Majs William Dalton and his 'Bear' James Graham (in 'Otter 02' 63-8329). Their leader, Maj Robert Huntley and Capt Ralph Stearman (in 63-8320), had already hit a MiG, although their kill claim was later rejected. 'Otter 02' first encountered Moore and McKinney's damaged MiG-17 when it threatened Huntley, Dalton recalling, 'I closed as much as I could and started tracking and fired. I fired a short burst but was not tracking him, so I let up on the trigger, repositioned the pipper ahead of the MiG, let him fly up to it and tracked him. Again I opened fire, and as verified by my gun camera, I observed impacts on the left wing and left fuselage under the cockpit'.

At the same time, Capt Philip M Drew and Maj William Wheeler (in 63-8317) were told of two MiG-17s on their tail, and they made a hard 180-degree turn into them, approaching one from behind. 'I had no problem tracking him, so I continued my attack, firing 756 rounds of 20 mm until I could see the end of the MiG's wing tips on each side of the canopy bow, which put him about 100 ft away', Drew explained. 'Prior to breaking off my attack I saw numerous 20 mm rounds impacting in his fuselage and right wing-root. As I crossed over him I saw the aircraft markings on the top of his left wing'.

Like Moore, Drew was unable to ascertain the victim's fate as other MiGs were all around, and he was forced to descend to 50 ft to shake one off, at which point he saw the smoke plume of a crashed jet on the ground.

Although no more MiGs fell to Thunderchief units, F-105G 62-4424 of the 17th WWS was downed by MiG-21 pilot Ngo Van Phu on 11 May 1972. Majs William Talley and James Padgett were captured.

WILD WEASELS

From the earliest *Iron Hand* strikes by F-105Ds in July 1965, the Thunderchief was increasingly directed against North Vietnam's most sophisticated weapons – its surface-to-air missiles. Initially, the only defence available to crews targeting SAMs was to attack them from extremely low altitudes, hazarding the punishing small-arms and AAA fire that protected such high value sites. Indeed, many batteries were actually flak traps, complete with dummy 'Fan Song' units and launchers, but with plenty of real AAA focused on the jets' predictable attack routes.

From August 1965 it was realised that specialised hunter-killer teams with effective ECM equipment would be needed to combat this serious threat to US air operations over the North. The teams included a 'pathfinder' jet to locate and mark active SAM sites and F-105 bombers to destroy them in low-altitude attacks.

Initially, four F-100Fs were modified to carry an ATI Vector IV (AN/APR-25) RHAW set and IR-133 panoramic S-band receiver in a project code-named *Wild Weasel I*. Crews trained as pairs (like most subsequent *Weasels)* initially under Maj Garry Willard. Capt Allen Lamb flew the first successful *Wild Weasel* mission on 22 December 1965 after a training period marked by trial and error, as he explained to the author;

'There was no training to speak of for *Wild Weasel I*. It was "cut and paste" to see if it would work. We did a run against the surface-to-air defence system at Eglin AFB, Florida, to check the accuracy of the equipment. Then we went to war to see if it would really work. Each crew did its own thing.'

Lamb's first SAM site kill, on 22 December, with Capt Jack Donovan involved four 421st TFS F-105Ds as 'Spruce' flight, led by Don Langwell. Capt Lamb, as 'Spruce 5', homed in on the heavily camouflaged site, lining up at low altitude to mark it for the F-105s to attack. After the lead element of the flight had fired their 2.75-inch rockets, Art Brattkus ('Spruce 4') made his attack. He recalled;

'We were moving smartly up the Red River in radio silence when up ahead I saw Allen Lamb pop up and then roll in way too close to the ground. I thought to myself that he was going to mark the target with his aircraft. I spotted a structure that wasn't burning and threw some rockets at it, pulled off to the right to get out of Al's way and damned near hit another "Thud". As I pulled out I saw several SAMs under their camouflage and threw all the rest of my rockets in their direction.'

In all 304 rockets and 2900 rounds of 20 mm ammunition were used for that first successful attack.

A second *Wild Weasel I* mission was made in mid-February 1966, led by Maj Bob Krone (469th TFS Operations Officer). It still used the five-ship formation, with four F-105Ds struggling to stay with the slower F-100F at 400 knots. The third strike, which saw a SAM training site near Hanoi attacked with new napalm/white phosphorous bombs and 19-shot rocket pods, apparently caused the deaths of several Soviet advisors.

Maj Bob Krone flew on the second SAM site attack with Allen Lamb in mid-February 1966. Two weeks earlier, on 31 January, he had led a 469th TFS mission that saw his flight exclusively penetrate appalling weather and attack barges under low cloud. Squadronmate Capt Eugene Hamilton perished when his aircraft (61-0210) was downed by AAA near Vinh shortly after attacking the barges (*USAF*)

Wild Weasel I missions continued nevertheless, while two F-105Ds were modified with Vector IV as *Wild Weasel II* project aircraft. This venture was quickly shelved and a new project was begun which added radar homing capability to the radar warning AN/APR-25 fit.

Seven F-105Fs were selected to use the same reliable AN/APR-25, AN/APR-26 and IR-133 avionics as fitted in the *Wild Weasel I* F-100Fs. The *Wild Weasel III* set-up included AN/APR-25 (Vector IV) threat displays in both cockpits and a CRT and hand controls in the rear cockpit for the IR-133, which required two flush-mounted antennas on the fuselage sides and a third under the nose. The ATI AN/APR-26 launch warning set intercepted the guidance signals between the SA-2 and its 'Fan Song' radar, registering sudden power increases in the signal that would indicate an imminent launch about 40 seconds later. Later, the AN/APR-25/26 was modified by Takhli ECM 'guru' Airman Weldon Bauman to show the direction of actual SAM launch strobes, rather than a range of unprioritised threat signals.

The F-105F carried more ordnance than the F-100F, including the AGM-45 Shrike anti-radiation missile, although some pilots felt that guns or cluster bomb units were the best weapons against SAM sites.

Flight-testing with the prototype *Wild Weasel* F-105F (62-4416) began in February 1966, and seven aircraft were ready by 18 March, despite many avionics problems. Six more were completed by late May 1966 for deployment to Korat, but their introduction was delayed when the USAF decided to fit them with the ATI AE-100 azimuth-elevation terminal homing system. The latter device showed the approximate location of a SAM site's radar transmissions as a green dot in the pilot's optical sight. Jets fitted with 'az-el' equipment had four small log periodic antennas visible aft of the radome. A further warning system called QRC-317 SEE-SAMS, which showed when an aircraft was centred in a 'Fan Song's' sights, was also tested but initially rejected as unreliable.

Five *Wild Weasel* F-105Fs and eight crews were deployed in great secrecy to Korat on 22 May 1966. After several F-100F orientation flights, crews commenced operational missions into RP VI in early June.

The crew of F-105F 63-8327, assigned to the 44th TFS, prepare to taxi out at Korat in July 1969. Their pre-fight briefing usually began with a weather estimate, followed by a target briefing on up to three possibilities each, with its designator and 'success' code words, plus other code words to indicate SAMs and MiGs in the area. After this half-hour session, individual flight briefings were held by flight leaders dealing with bombing tactics and communications procedures, amongst other things, for a further 30 minutes. Crews then 'suited up' (including their 90 lbs of survival gear) and were driven to the flightline in a bus painted in the squadron colour. Like most F-105s, 63-8327 had been fitted with two reinforcing 'straps' across its bomb-bay doors by the time this photograph was taken (*USAF*)

The first 'radar kill' was achieved on the 7th of that month when a GCI site was hit by 2.75-inch rockets. Despite having given the aircraft its combat debut, the pilots involved were still not allowed to know much about the *Weasels'* capabilities.

By mid-June *Weasels* were operating close to Hanoi, hitting several 'Fan Songs' and destroying at least one SAM site while escorting the big 29 June Hanoi POL strike.

The first Air Force Cross for a *Weasel* crew was awarded to Majs Bill Robinson and Peter Tsouprake, who badly damaged four SAM sites during Hanoi area strikes on 5 July. Sadly, the first *Weasel* crew to be lost

A Takhli armament crew check yet another load of M117s for F-105F 63-8351 *The Kad* of the 354th TFS. Shrikes are already in place. The stresses of combat caught up with this *Weasel* in June 1976 when structural cracks in the wings caused it to be written off while serving as an F-105G-1-RE with the 35th TFW (*USAF via C Moggeridge*)

went down in 13th TFS F-105F 63-8286 'Pepper 01' the very next day when the jet was hit by 57 mm AAA during an *Iron Hand* near Thai Nguyen. The EWO, Capt Charles Morgan, was one of the few black airmen lost over the North, and although he was captured, no more was heard of either him or his pilot, Maj Roosevelt Hestle.

Many equipment variations (including an upgraded SEE-SAMS B set) were operationally tested in these early aircraft, which were sometimes unofficially called 'EF-105Fs'.

A second batch of six jets and eight crews were sent to Korat later in June as Project *Wild Weasel III-2*, but on 3 July they were transferred to Takhli, beginning operations on the 10th. When the F-100F detachment ended on 11 July, Korat's F-105Fs became a flight within the recently activated 13th TFS, and the squadron's F-105Ds were used mainly in *Weasel*-led *Iron Hand* flights. Twelve F-105Fs were on strength by September, with only one loss, and the unit's anti-SAM role expanded in 1967 with the introduction of *Commando Nail* missions. Ultimately, the 388th TFW was forced by attrition to consolidate as a three-squadron wing, losing the 13th TFS on 21 October 1967, while its F-105 activities at Korat passed to the 44th TFS until 15 October 1969. At that point the unit flew a mix of F-105D/F aircraft in strike and *Weasel* roles.

At Takhli, rather than joining a single unit within the 355th TFW, the *Weasels* had been assigned as a fifth ('E') flight, boasting some of the most experienced F-105 pilots, to each of the wing's three squadrons beginning with the 354th TFS on 4 July 1966. They flew *Iron Hand* against active SA-2 sites in the path of the bomber force (following 30 miles behind), then hunter-killer activities, seeking and destroying SAM sites near the target. Col Broughton preferred Korat's single unit approach, however;

'We were almost always short on *Weasel* aircraft and crews. I wanted one *Weasel* guy to manage the assets and call the shots. At Takhli I had a super smart, aggressive good guy *Weasel* leader in Leo Thorsness.'

The expertise of the 13th TFS at Korat was invaluable in refining tactics and dealing with the frequent modifications to the *Weasel* avionics for crews who had received only six weeks' training on the aircraft at

Maj John Dudash and Capt Alton Meyer were shot down by a SAM in F-105F 63-8277 during a Thai Nguyen thermal plant attack on 26 April 1967 – the same day that US Navy Iron Hand pioneer Lt Cdr Michael Estocin (the only US Navy jet pilot to be awarded the Medal of Honor) was also lost in his A-4E. SA-2s were often fired in threes, and Dudash had managed to evade the first two missiles. 63-8277's ordnance here includes an AGM-45 Shrike and a CBU-24 cluster bomb for SAM site attacks. In combat, *Wild Weasel* aircraft with weapons aboard could only avoid oncoming SAMs by making hard, turning dives into them. Acceleration could be gained only by diving, and repeated missile evasion manoeuvres took the F-105s to ever-lower altitudes, increasing their exposure to groundfire. On long escort missions such as the one being flown by these jets, aircrew were often grateful for the F-105's 'home comforts', as Murray Denton recalled. 'It had a relief tube which we needed for missions with B-52s requiring multiple drops by the "Buffs". Some missions would require four refuelling and four different times on target' (*Capt Paul Chesley via Jim Rotramel*)

Nellis AFB. Tactics were largely devised in the field on the premise that low-altitude attacks offered the best protection, although the low-altitude parameters of the SA-2 were not really known – several crews reported SAMs tracking and pursuing their aircraft at altitudes below 200 ft.

Weasels set up two separate orbits to 'troll' near the SAM site, arranged so that one element was usually pointing at the potential threat. Essentially, they were there to draw the fire of the SAM sites off the strikers, evading missiles with the standard technique of a split-S dive followed by a reverse split-S climb, using more 'g' than the SA-2 could match. Careful timing and steely nerves were vital as three SAMs were usually launched simultaneously.

Most EWOs were volunteers, many coming from SAC postings, while pilots tended to be senior 'high time' flyers. Initial losses were heavy, with four of the six 354th TFS *Weasels* being shot down between 23 July and 17 August 1966 at a time of heavy attrition for the wing generally. Majs Gene Pemberton and Ben Newsom in 'Drill 01' (63-8338) were the first to go when a barrage of SA-2s hit their F-105F and severely damaged their wingman's jet. The crew's fate is unknown, but F-105D pilot Capt Buddy Reinbold, although seriously wounded, recovered his jet despite it suffering 87 shrapnel holes and losing the top of its vertical stabiliser.

Two *Weasels* were destroyed on 'Black Sunday', 7 August. 63-8358, with Capts Ed Larson and K A 'Mike' Gilroy aboard, was hit by a SAM which exploded their gun's ammunition drum, blowing the nose off the aircraft and filling the cockpit with stifling smoke. Incredibly, the crippled F-105, with hydraulic fluid streaming out, a massive hole in the wing and the top of the fin shot away, got the crew out over the coast for a recovery by HU-16 amphibian. The F-105 exploded seconds after they had ejected. Minutes later 63-8361, following up with two Shrikes and two rocket pods, was crippled by an 85 mm hit, forcing Capts Robert Sandvick and Thomas Shaw to eject.

That day, five F-105s were among eight US aerial losses. Only one *Weasel* remained at Takhli. The two surviving crews were temporarily transferred to Korat, returning to Takhli in October to fly with replacement crews that included Capts Jerry Hoblit and Merle Dethlefsen and Maj Leo Thorsness.

A further batch of 18 *Weasels* was pushed through modification at the Sacramento Air Materiel Centre (SMAMA), followed by 36 more in November 1966 and 19 in June 1967, bringing the total number of these invaluable assets to 86. These aircraft had an ER-142 panoramic receiver with two scopes in place of the IR-133. Increased numbers meant two *Weasels* could be assigned to each *Iron Hand* flight.

To reduce attrition the tactics changed from primary, but loss-prone, *Iron Hand* site attacks to electronic suppression of the SAM radars, preventing the missiles from being launched by jamming their guidance systems. The introduction of Shrike missiles also gave limited stand-off capability, followed up by CBU-24s or M117s delivered from higher, safer altitudes than had been required with the earlier gun and rocket attacks. By mid-1967 there were at least 18 active SAM sites in Hanoi's defensive ring, and a good 'bear' (EWO) had to monitor them all if possible, plus the 'Firecan' AAA gun radars and 'Barlock' GCI radars guiding MiGs. He also had to combine the roles of navigator, EWO and weapons systems officer (WSO).

However, additional self-protection was still needed for the *Weasels*, without having to use external pylons for ECM pods. Development of various jammers starting with the QRC-301 (a version of the US Navy's AN/ALQ-5) was undertaken from 1966 and tested on the sides of the F-105F's outer pylons. A version of the Westinghouse QRC-288 deception jamming pod was then combined with elements of the QRC-335 as the QRC-380 (later AN/ALQ-105) and spilt between two blister mountings on the F-105F's centre fuselage. Added to this were a Borders QRC-373 acquisition radar jamming system and an AN/APR-35 panoramic and analysis receiver. None of these systems, however, could give the accurate location of a SAM radar from long range (risky over-flight of the source was required for this), or of the distance between the F-105 and its target radar. Target photographs were seldom good enough to identify sites visually either.

The final major development in the evolution of the definitive F-105 *Wild Weasel* was the acquisition of a better anti-radar missile. The US Navy-developed AGM-45A Shrike had provided some successes, combined with CBU-24s or rockets, but its small 145-lb frangible warhead and short range (typically around six miles, compared with 17 miles for an SA-2 with a 400-lb warhead and 3600 shrapnel pieces) were handicaps because the launching F-105 was always in range of a SAM. Also, the enemy could defeat Shrikes by turning radars briefly to 'standby' when a missile was launched, breaking its lock. 'Lofting' several missiles from high altitude could reduce the chances of detection by 'Fan Song' operators, but it also diminished the Shrike's accuracy at a time when its success rate was only about 15 per cent. Hits were hard to see and pilots

F-105F *Wild Weasels* were soon regarded as essential for all RP VI missions. Here, 63-8347, serving with the 44th TFS in 1969, has the 75 ft of 9 x 3 inch film in its strike camera replaced. The camera photographed the target 'fore and aft' when the bomb release was pressed. Named *Dragon II* whilst with the 388th TFW at Korat, it moved to the 44th TFS at Takhli in May 1970, where it was renamed *Mt Ida Flash/Honky Tonk Woman*. Subsequently withdrawn to McConnell AFB for F-105G updates, 63-8347 returned to combat with the 17th WWS. On 17 May 1972 the aircraft landed overweight at Korat after an aborted mission, blew a tyre and burned itself out when it ran off the runway. The crew escaped without injury (*USAF*)

usually measured the missile's flight time, noting if a radar signal went off the air at the end of that time.

To improve the situation General Dynamics developed its naval Standard Type 1A surface-to-air missile to operate as an air-launched anti-radar weapon, the AGM-78A (Mod 0) Standard ARM. This model, set up by the EWO and fired by the pilot, used the Shrike seeker-head for expediency, combined with a much larger Aerojet Mk 27 motor that gave the missile a launch range longer than the SA-2's. Its 214-lb fragmentation warhead provided real destructive power, but its main

A 15-ft long AGM-78A Standard ARM is seen suspended from its special launch adapter on the pylon of test F-105G 63-8305. The missile became a high-priority project from 10 January 1967, with tests at Holloman AFB and White Sands Missile Range beginning in August of that year. The Mach 2.5 AGM-78 could be launched from a distance of up to 35 miles from the target – well outside SA-2 range. At 1365 lbs, it weighed far more than the 390-lb Shrike, and it could be launched at targets up to 170 degrees off the F-105's direction of travel (*USAF*)

innovation was its programmable capability and gimballed antenna which could re-acquire emissions if a 'Fan Song' shut down.

As a US Navy project, the AGM-78A's combat debut was undertaken on A-6B 'Mod 0 Update' Intruders. Cdr Phil Waters, who made some of the earliest combat launches, explained;

'The Standard ARM had several different launch modes depending on launch circumstances which made it more flexible than the Shrike. It could be programmed to turn to a certain bearing after launch and then seek to acquire a target. The crew had absolutely no control of the missile after launch, but if it had been locked on to a radar that subsequently shut down it would continue to guide to the last known location of the radar. This might not ensure a hit, but it was an improvement over the Shrike, which would have gone its own way when the radar was shut down.'

Modification of 14 F-105Fs began at SMAMA in September 1967 to add the AGM-78A to their *Wild Weasel* equipment. Deliveries to the 357th TFS at Takhli commenced later that year, with the unit having eight Mod 0 F-105Fs on strength by February 1968. The missile made its USAF combat debut on 10 March when four 357th TFS 'Barracuda' flight F-105Fs, led by Maj Harlan Wyman and Capt Ron Davenport, fired eight AGM-78As at SA-2 sites near the Ha Dong army barracks. Although the first missile fell away because its motor ignition lanyard was detached, five out of the remaining seven weapons guided successfully and three 'Fan Songs' could be confirmed as destroyed.

Further USAF AGM-78A operations were curtailed by the bombing halt on 1 April, and the emphasis for the *Weasels* shifted to the 'trails' war and support for B-52 *Arc Light* missions.

WILIEST *WEASEL*

SMAMA, meanwhile, had started work on the next *Weasel* upgrade of 16 F-105Fs to give them AGM-78B/C Mod 1 capability. This revised missile did not require seeker tuning before launch, enabling it to engage targets of opportunity. Most components in the F-105Fs' electronic warfare suite were upgraded too, including the fitment of an AN/APR-35 panoramic receiver in place of the ER-142, AN/APR-36 and -37 replacing the AN/APR-25 and -26 and a new missile control panel with 14-channel tape recorder and bomb-damage assessment system.

New jets were delivered from January 1969 as 'Mod 1' F-105Fs, and the USAF decided ten months later to bring all *Weasel* Thunderchiefs up to this standard, giving them the new designation F-105G. Another dozen F-105Fs were also added to the modification line. Late in this process the configuration of the QRC-380 and AN/ALQ-105 ECM suites was confirmed, and this 'Class V' addition was made to the F-105G as standard. In practice, use of the AN/ALQ-105 was limited as it interfered with the aircraft's electronic receivers, although it could be interrupted by the pilot. The system's noise-jamming mode was useful in deflecting an approaching SAM, nevertheless.

The AGM-45 Shrike was also retained for the F-105G, and a dual launcher asymmetrical adapter was developed by the US Navy. Two LAU-34/A Mod 1 launchers could now be fitted on either outboard pylon, thus increasing the missile load to six, including two AGM-78s. A more typical installation was a pair of single-launcher Shrikes, plus a single AGM-78 on the right inboard pylon balanced on the left by a drop tank. Col Dan Barry, who flew with the 44th and 561st TFSs, remembered;

'I don't ever recall flying a jet with the dual Shrike launcher, and it seems that our aeroplanes may not have had that modification. I did fly at least one mission with two AGM-78s and two AGM-45s, however. This was a very unusual load since your only fuel was internal and in the 650-gallon centreline tank. You would be overweight to take-off if there was fuel in the latter, and we were prohibited from taking off with partial fuel in it. This meant that you had to get to the tanker quickly after take-off. If there had been any refuelling problems it would have been necessary to jettison those very expensive AGM-78s for a minimum-fuel landing. This did not happen, everything went as planned and I came down "Thud Ridge" with that missile load feeling like a 1000-lb gorilla!'

F-105F 62-4444 was the fifth *Combat Martin* conversion, and the jet was later upgraded to F-105G-1-RE standard. It is seen here in 17th WWS service (*USAF via A Thornborough*)

F-105F 63-311 *SAM FIGHTER* from the 354thth TFS/355th TFW was assigned to Maj Bill Scott and Capt Cliff Gollino and maintained by Sgts Young, McDonald, Mayfield and Reader. It is seen here awaiting its next mission while on detachment to Da Nang in May 1970. Five successful SAM site attacks are marked up on its nose. The jet's luck ran out six months later on 15 November when it crashed following engine failure during an escort mission. The crew safely ejected (*USAF*)

'We also went through a period when we had to give up a Shrike station to carry a recorder the wing was using to try and pick up some SAM guidance signals. When carrying just a single AGM-78, the common practice was to feed the wing tank down to the point where the aileron trim was neutral, then you quit feeding from that tank. Being in trim, the jet was cleaner, and when you launched the missile it didn't affect the aircraft's balance too much thanks to the partially full wing tank, which you then selected and fed out. I was reluctant to jettison any tanks because there were documented incidents of them coming off "squirrely" and hitting the aeroplane, either causing damage or actually knocking the jet down. I also liked to keep the tanks in case we rolled into a SAR mission, as you could hit the tanker and have some meaningful fuel to work with. A clean F-105 just didn't have much range.'

Fellow *Wild Weasel* pilot Maj Murray Denton added;

'The asymmetric trim was no problem in flight, but if we didn't expend the AGM-78 on the mission, which was the case on many sorties, we later found out that when we got back to base we were technically "out of limits" for landing. We were just lucky I guess!'

As the war moved back into Laos and South Vietnam the *Weasel* role was reduced, as Col Barry explained;

'My first combat mission was on 26 January 1970 flying the D-model. For the remainder of the time at Takhli I flew a mix of Ds and Gs. There was a period when we flew the F-105Gs on strike missions just like a D, often in Laos where there was no EW threat, but we always had an EWO in the back seat. The F-105Gs were restricted from flying strike missions as they were a limited asset, and there was concern about losing them.'

F-105Gs arrived at Takhli from mid-1969, but the inactivation of the 355th TFW in October 1970 caused their transfer to Korat. Initially labelled Det 1 of the 12th TFS, this unit became the 6010th WWS on 1 November 1970. One of its first pilots was Col Dan Barry;

'I remember that we were all a bit puzzled when we learned that we were going to be in the 6010th WWS – a number totally foreign to any historical fighter unit designation. Since this was during the "drawing down" in Southeast Asia, I remember thinking it was probably a ploy to conceal a combat organisation by giving us a designation that looked more like a number you would associate with some kind of support activity such as a base exchange!'

The squadron was led by Lt Col Gus Sonderman, a former World War 2 fighter pilot. One of its most daring, and potentially historic, contributions to the conflict came on 21 November 1970 when it participated in the daring attempt to free PoWs from the Son Tay camp, where 47 EWOs were among the captives. Five *Wild Weasels* were the 'leading edge' of an operation involving 116 aircraft that went exactly to plan, except that the prisoners had been moved from the camp due to water supply problems. F-105G 62-4436, flown by Maj Don Kilgus and Capt Ted Lowry, was hit by SA-2 shrapnel and the crew ejected when fuel rapidly drained from holed tanks. They were rescued by one of the HH-53s that intended to bring back the PoWs. 'Firebird 4' was flown by Maj Murray Denton and his 'Bear' Capt Russ Ober, the former recalling;

'We were told by Lt Col Sonderman about a possible mission two or three days previously, and ordered to stay at Korat until we knew more details. Lt Col Kronebusch and his "Bear" deployed to Takhli to brief and plan the mission. We were not told of the actual mission until about six hours prior to take-off. We flew F-105G 63-8306 with two Shrikes and three fuel tanks. "Firebird 3" was hit 30-45 minutes after TOT (time on target). He egressed to the west and recovered at Udorn. "Firebird 5" (Kilgus/Lowry) assumed "Firebird 3's" orbit and was hit about 20 minutes later. Maj Kilgus thought it was a only a near miss and stayed in orbit until "Apple" (HH-53 rescue force) was egressing Son Tay.

'We departed toward Udorn, and shortly thereafter Kilgus saw that he was about out of fuel and declared an emergency. I asked for a vector to the nearest tanker, refuelled and headed back towards the bailout area. Kilgus and Lowry had ejected near the Plain of Jars in Laos. Shortly thereafter I was advised that "Apple 5" was recovering the aircrew and I could return to Udorn. All ordnance was expended and the "spooks" gave us credit for four SAM sites destroyed and one damaged.'

Russ Ober's log book records 3.3 hours flying time that day. The 'Son Tay Raiders' provided a powerful demonstration of America's commitment to its PoWs at a time when morale was low.

Other missions flown by the 6010th WWS focused on 'protective reaction' strikes against AAA sites that had fired at US reconnaissance flights. One of its early missions was codenamed Operation *Louisville Slugger*, which saw a series of SAM site attacks in the Ban Karai Pass in December 1970, followed by a similar series of strikes in Operation *Fraction Cross Alpha* in March 1971.

The 6010th WWS was replaced by the 17th WWS on 1 December 1971, and its 15 F-105Gs continued to deal with the increasing number of SAM sites and radar-controlled AAA on the trails network near the Laotian border. These sites were a particular threat to B-52 *Arc Light* missions, and *Wild Weasel* support was required for many of them. Lt Col Scott McIntire flew as 'Ashcan 02' in a two-ship *Weasel* operation near the Mu Gia Pass on 10 December. Several Shrikes were fired at a site but his aircraft (63-8426) took a SAM hit at 18,000 ft. EWO Maj Robert Belli 'command ejected' the crew and was rescued but McIntire perished.

The unit was involved in support of Operation *Proud Deep Alpha* against the increasing SAM network that month as the North Vietnamese prepared for their major incursion into South Vietnam. F-105G 63-8333, was lost to a SAM on 17 February 1972 and Capts J Cutter and K Fraser were captured despite ejecting four miles out to sea.

When full-scale hostilities recommenced in April 1972, the 17th WWS was the only *Weasel* unit in-theatre. Missions against POL and storage sites close to Hanoi and Haiphong were scheduled once again in the *Freedom Train* campaign in support of tactical and B-52 attacks, merging in April 1972 with the start of the *Linebacker I* period. New tactics included hunter-killer teamwork with F-4Es against targets in the

North and defences that had been massively reinforced during four-year bombing halt. There were now 300+ SAM and 1500+ AAA sites north of the DMZ. F-105G 63-8342 was lost on 6 April with Capts Paul Mateja and Orvin Jones during *Iron Hand* support for a 17-aircraft B-52 missions against POL and SAM storage sites near Haiphong. Although 250 missiles were launched, this was the only USAF loss.

The following day the over-tasked 17th WWS received some much needed support at Korat when recently formed Det 1 of the 561st TFS/23rd TFW arrived from McConnell AFB as part of Operation *Constant Guard 1*. The 561st had been divided into two echelons, Advance and Rear, upon its formation earlier in the year, and it was the Advance group of 12 F-105Gs that flew into Korat from 7 April in the wake of the North Vietnamese Easter Offensive. Col Dan Barry was with them;

'While we shared our ops building with the 17th WWS, we tried to keep our operations separate. When the daily "frag" came in the schedulers (of which I was one) would get together and equitably split the sorties to keep them equal on nights versus days, route packages, etc., based on the number of jets and crews each unit had. There was the usual rivalry, but we were pretty much equal partners, particularly as we were TDY. Shortly after our arrival our CO, Ed Rock, was named 17th WWS CO and our Ops Officer, Dick Moser, moved up to become 561st CO.

'When the 561st deployed to Korat our first loss was on 11 May when pilot Bill Talley and EWO Jim Padgett were downed in 62-4424 by Ngo Duy Thu, and both ended up as PoWs. Bill told me he didn't know that he'd been shot down by a MiG-21 until after he was released. He never saw it, and thought he'd had some kind of catastrophic engine failure.'

A 182-mission veteran, Talley had been unexpectedly returned to flight status on the day he was shot down, having actually been scheduled to return to the USA and retire. Two more losses occurred in September, the first of these involving Capt Tom Zorn and 1Lt Mike Turose on 17 September. Ejecting from 63-8360 over water after it had been damaged by a SAM north of Haiphong, both men drowned before they could be recovered. Twelve days later squadron CO Lt Col James O'Neill

F-105F 63-8302 *Half a Yard/Jefferson Airplane* was assigned to Lt Col Ed Moriarty of the 44th TFS in 1970. As 'Crow 01' on 29 September 1972, Lt Col James O'Neil and Capt M J Bosiljevak were hit by a SAM near Phuc Yen when they tried to set up a Shrike launch against the site. Both crew ejected and a rescue effort was frustrated by MiG intervention. Only Lt Col O'Neil survived imprisonment (*USAF via Norm Taylor*)

and Capt Michael Bosiljevac were also hit by an SA-2 in 63-8302, and although O'Neil survived as a PoW, his EWO perished.

The end of *Linebacker I* on 22 October brought no let-up in *Wild Weasel* activity while the abortive negotiations continued in Paris. The last Thunderchief to fall to enemy action in Southeast Asia was lost on 16 November, and Col Dan Barry was involved in the rescue efforts;

'Capt Ken Theate and Maj Norman Maier from the 561st were shot down by a SAM and I was the *Wild Weasel* lead on the rescue effort. I was airborne for more than nine hours, and I remember on one refuelling a tanker came way north over Laos, as it was questionable whether we were going to be able to make it back to the emergency recovery runway at Nakhon Phanom. A-7Ds had taken over the search and rescue role from the A-1 on this very day, and they did a great job in trying circumstances.'

The SAM that hit Theate and Maier's F-105G (63-8359) emerged from cloud without warning while they were flying as a B-52 escort. The explosion blew a hole in the jet's nose and rendered the crew unconscious for about two minutes before they punched out near Dong Xuon and hid overnight. The rescue effort the next day involved 356th TFS A-7Ds, with Maj Arnie Clark giving the type its debut as a replacement for the aged A-1 'Sandys'.

Clark managed to penetrate thick, low cloud and locate the F-105G crew for the successful HH-53 rescuers. He was airborne for a total of nine hours thanks to four aerial refuellings, and it sustained AAA damage. Clark was awarded the Air Force Cross for his persistence.

When bombing resumed in *Linebacker II* on 18 December, 17th WWS crews each flew up to three missions a day to support the incessant bombardment of the North by B-52s at night and tactical aircraft around the clock. Most of the unit's nocturnal missions were *Iron Hand*, and these were flown intensively, but without losses. Single *Weasels* patrolled a set orbit between the B-52s and the SAM sites, using careful timing to avoid the deluge of bombs from 'Buffs' flying 30,000 ft above them.

On the first night, 18 December, Capt Don Henry and EWO Maj Bob Webb destroyed three SAM sites with an AGM-78 and two Shrikes, the latter fired head-on at a site that was aiming three SA-2s directly at them. Almost 900 SAMs were fired at the B-52 force during the 11-day onslaught, and losses could have greatly exceeded the 15 downed aircraft without such effective *Weasel* suppression work. President Nixon's rapid decision to pursue *Linebacker II* had meant that there was no time to organise a softening up of the defences before the bombing began.

After the painfully achieved peace treaty, strike support sorties into Laos continued until 21 February 1973, and the 561st TFS returned to the USA seven months later. The last 17th WWS jet did not leave Thailand until 29 October 1974.

F-105G 62-4225 *Kloyjai* returns to Korat RTAFB on 29 December 1972 at the conclusion of the final *Wild Weasel* mission of Operation *Linebacker II*. Capts Jim Boyd and Kim Pepperell obviously found no targets for their Shrike missiles, since North Vietnam's defences had been substantially neutralised by then (*USAF*)

APPENDICES

F-105 DEPLOYMENTS TO THAILAND AND SOUTH VIETNAM

4th TFW, Seymour Johnson AFB, North Carolina

334th TFS – TDY to Takhli 28 August 1965 (6235th TFW). To 355th TFW, TDY 8 November 1965 to early February 1966.
335th TFS – To Yokota 3 July 1965, supporting 6441st units rotating to Takhli. To Takhli, 6235th TFW, 3 November to 15 December 1965.

18th TFW, Kadena AB, Okinawa

12th TFS – To Da Nang as Det 2, 18th TFW, TDY 25 December 1964. Squadron to Korat, via Da Nang, 1 February to 15 March. To Korat 15 June to 25 August 1965. Augmented Korat *Wild Weasel* operations, summer 1968.
44th TFS – First F-105s to Thailand 20-30 April 1964. At Da Nang (Det 2, 18th TFW) and Korat from 18 December 1964 to 25 February 1965. To 6234th TFW, Korat, 21 April to 23 June and 10 to 29 October 1965.
67th TFS – To Da Nang as Det 2, 18th TFW. To Korat TDY 18 February, transferring to 6234th TFW 5-26 April 1965. To Korat 16 August to 23 October 1965.

23rd TFW, McConnell AFB, Kansas

561st TFS – To Yokota 27 February 1965, rotating to Takhli from 6 April to 10 July 1965.
562nd TFS – To Takhli 6 August to 4 December 1965.
563rd TFS – To Takhli 7 April to 15 August 1965.

41st AD/6441st TFW, Yokota AB, Japan

35th TFS – To Korat 24 September to 20 November 1964. To Takhli (6235th TFW) 4 May to 26 June 1965 and 19 October to 15 November 1965.
36th TFS – To Korat 12 August to 5 October 1964. To Takhli 6 March to 4 May 1965 and 17 August to 28 October 1965.
80th TFS – To Korat 30 October to 29 December 1964. To Takhli 27 June to 26 August 1965.

355th TFW, Takhli RTAFB, Thailand (*replaced 6235th TFW, which managed Takhli deployments 8 April to 8 November 1965*)

44th TFS – Reassigned from 388th TFW, 15 October 1969 to 6 October 1970.
333rd TFS – Reassigned PCS from 4th TFW, 8 December 1965 to 15 October 1970.
354th TFS – To Kadena 3 March 1965, with rotations to Korat. Whole unit to Korat by April 1965 (6234th TFW). Relocated PCS to Takhli 27 November 1965 to 14 December 1970.
357th TFS – To Yokota 5 August 1964. To Korat 12 June to 20 August 1965. PCS to 355th TFW, Takhli, until 10 December 1970.
469th TFS – To Kadena TDY 30 November 1964, rotating to Korat from 5 January to 13 March 1965. To 6234th TFW at Korat 8 November 1965 as first PCS F-105 unit in Southeast Asia.

388th TFW, Korat RTAFB, Thailand (*replaced 6234th TFW, which managed Korat TDYs 5 April 1965 to 8 April 1966*)

Det 1, 12th TFS (*became 6010th WWS*) – 1 November 1970 to December 1971. To Korat (as 17th WWS) 1 December 1971 to 16 May 1972.
13th TFS – Formed from 44th TFS, 15 May 1966 to 18 October 1967.
17th WWS – Replaced 6010th WWS, 1 December 1971 to 15 November 1974.
34th TFS – 15 May 1966 to May 1969 (when transitioned to F-4E).
44th TFS – Reformed from the 421st TFS 25 April 1967. Absorbed 13th TFS 18 October 1967. To 355th TFW 15 October 1969.
421st TFS – From 6234th TFW 8 April 1966 to 25 April 1967.
469th TFS – From 6234th TFS 8 April 1966 to 17 November 1968 (when transitioned to F-4E).
Det 1, 561st TFS – 12 April 1972 to 10 September 1973.
6010th WWS – 1 November 1970 to 1 December 1971.

COLOUR PLATES

1

F-105D-25-RE 61-0217 of the 12th TFS/18th TFW, Korat RTAFB, Thailand, March 1965
The 12th TFS/18th TFW participated in the first PACAF F-105 deployment as a unit of the 18th TFW from the spring of 1963. Amongst the first examples issued to the wing, 61-0217 flew *Barrel Roll* and early *Rolling Thunder* missions with the 12th TFS in 1964. When the unit returned to Kadena AB on 25 August 1965 many of its aircraft remained at Korat with the 67th TFS. Lt Col Robinson Risner, architect of the first attacks on the Than Hoa 'Dragon's Jaw' Bridge, was shot down in this aircraft on 16 September 1965. Hit by AAA during an early SAM site attack he ejected near Thanh Hoa and spent the remainder of the war as a PoW.

2

F-105D-31-RE 62-4408 of the 561st TFS/23rd TFW (6235th TFW), Takhli RTAFB, Thailand, May 1965
This aircraft has Project *Look Alike* aluminised lacquer paint with buzz numbers and 30-inch fuselage insignia, but it lacks a strike camera, ECM or the cooling air-scoops on the rear fuselage. Pods for 2.75-inch rockets are carried, however. The 561st TFS received F-105Ds in late 1963, and it subsequently became the first 23rd TFW unit to deploy under Operation *One Buck Nine* from McConnell AFB to Yokota AB for SIOP (nuclear alert) duties between 27 February and 10 July 1965. From 6 April a third of the squadron rotated to Takhli RTAFB, giving most of its pilots combat experience in the 70 missions flown before returning to McConnell AFB. This F-105D was lost with its pilot, Capt Robert Wistrand, on 9 May 1965 while strafing during a *Steel Tiger* armed reconnaissance sortie over the Mu Gia Pass. Wistrand was hit while strafing a AAA site and did not eject from the diving aircraft.

3

F-105D-20-RE 61-0116 of the 562nd TFS/23rd TFW (6235th TFW), Takhli RTAFB, Thailand, 1 September 1965
This aircraft is depicted after it had flown 50 combat missions, mostly with the 563rd TFS - it still bears the latter unit's markings, as the 562nd's rudder stripes were blue in colour. On 4 December 1965 61-0116 transferred to the 354th TFS/355th TFW at Takhli, and it was lost to AAA whilst serving with this unit on 20 July 1966 near Hanoi when Col William Nelson, a senior 355th TFW staff officer, made a second strafing run on a truck.

4

F-105D-31-RE 62-4347 of the 334th TFS/355th TFW, Takhli RTAFB, Thailand, November 1965
This aircraft was nicknamed *Little Lois Ann*, *Calamity Jane* and *Wendy June* in 355th TFW service from 29 July 1963 through to 24 October 1970. On 6 August 1964 it was among the 18 F-105Ds of the 357th TFS deployed to Yokota AB in response to the Gulf of Tonkin incident under Operation *One Buck Two*. 62-4347 then served at Kadena AB with the 469th TFS/355th TFW and the 421st TFS, prior to joining the 355th TFW at Takhli RTAFB on 12 March 1966. From there the jet flew combat missions for four years, regularly setting monthly sortie and flight-hours records without serious combat damage. Post-war, it served with the Kansas ANG's 184th TFTG until 28 March 1980, and then the 466th TFS, AFRES (including a *Coronet Rudder* deployment to Skrydstrup, Denmark), until retirement on 3 October 1983. The veteran jet took part in the final F-105 flypast at Hill AFB, decorated as the 'High Time Thud' in recognition of its 6730.5 flying hours - a record for the F-105. It was then put on permanent display at Hill AFB.

5

F-105D-31-RE 62-4379 of the 335th TFS/4th TFW (attached to the 355th TFW), Takhli RTAFB, Thailand, December 1965
This aircraft is depicted here as it appeared in the last week of the unit's TDY to Takhli from Yokota, which had begun on 3 November 1965. The 335th's aircraft were reassigned to the 333rd TFS from 5 December 1965 for *Barrel Roll* and *Steel Tiger* operations. 62-4379 was later passed on to the 421st TFS/388th TFW at Korat RTAFB. It was one of two F-105Ds from the squadron that were shot down within minutes of each other on 2 November 1966 over the North. Capt R F Loken was strafing a railway bridge when 62-4379 was hit by ground-fire. It flew him to a comparatively safe area of Laos before he had to bail out and return home by rescue helicopter. The jet is seen here carrying Mk 84 bombs.

6

F-105D-15-RE 61-0042 of the 357th TFS/355th TFW, Takhli RTAFB, Thailand, September 1966
The 357th TFS was assigned PCS to the 355th TFW from January 1965 after previous TDYs to Korat and Takhli. This aircraft has the 'reverse camouflage' applied to about a quarter of F-105s in late 1965, areas of FS 30219 Tan and FS 34012 Green being reversed from the standard pattern applied to most Thunderchiefs. 61-0042 was brought down by an 85 mm AAA shell while attacking the Vu Chua railway marshalling yard on 5 July 1967 - it was the third 355th TFW F-105 lost to AAA within the space of four minutes near Kep airfield on this date. Maj Ward Dodge ejected but died in prison about a week later from unknown causes. Between 17-31 May 1967, a period when mistreatment of prisoners was known to be particularly brutal, eight of the 21 airmen taken PoW in that time died in unexplained circumstances.

7

F-105D-5-RE 58-1168 *Betty's Boy* of the 354th TFS/355th TFW, Takhli RTAFB, Thailand, early 1967
This aircraft also has 'reverse camouflage', as well as an incorrectly marked serial, '81188'. *Betty's Boy* was being flown by Maj Jack Hunt as 'Nitro 01' when he shot down a MiG-17 during an attack on the Xuan Mai barracks on 19 April 1967. Hunt ordered the flight to jettison ordnance, after which both he and Maj Fred Tolman destroyed MiG-17s with 20 mm cannon fire. 58-1168 was subsequently lost during the successful 25 October 1967 attack on the Paul Doumer Bridge, Maj Gene 'Smitty' Smith, leading 'Wildcat' flight, being hit by 57 mm AAA. MiG-killer Capt G I Basel reported seeing the aircraft turn into 'a tumbling torch in the sky'. Injured during ejection and twice shot in the leg during capture, Maj Smith endured captivity until 14 March 1973.

8

F-105D-31-RE 62-4359 *12 O'Clock High* of the 421st TFS/388th TFW, Korat RTAFB, Thailand, April 1967
This aircraft has an early post-camouflage serial presentation, and is armed with six M117 bombs. It also has an AN/ALQ-71 pod on its outer starboard wing pylon. Later transferred to the 469th TFS, the jet was written off with the unit on 12 September 1968. Diverted to Takhli upon its return from a mission due to Korat being 'weathered out' and inaccessible, the F-105 ran out of fuel and crashed as no tanker was available. The pilot ejected safely.

9

F-105D-10-RE 60-0497 *Miss T* of the 44th TFS/388th TFW, Korat RTAFB, Thailand, June 1967
60-0497 was being flown by Maj 'Mo' Seaver (who later commanded the 347th TFW, flying the F-111) on 13 May 1967 when he shot down a MiG-17 with 20 mm cannon fire during a 90-second engagement. Six months later it was one of four F-105s lost on 18 November in an *Iron Hand* attack on the MiG base at Phuc Yen. Hit by a MiG-21's 'Atoll' missile, the Thunderchief took Lt Col William Reed back as far as Laos, where he ejected and was rescued near Pathet Lao troops. Here, the aircraft is seen fitted with a twin-Sidewinder launcher. Its MiG kill marking appeared on the left side of the forward fuselage.

10

F-105D-25-RE 61-0205 *MR BLACKBIRD* of the 34th TFS/388th TFW, Korat RTAFB, Thailand, Summer 1967
Assigned to Capt Anthony Andrews on 17 October 1967, this jet was one of three 34th TFS Thunderchiefs shot down within two minutes of each other whilst bombing the Dap Cau railway marshalling yards. 61-0205 took a 57 mm AAA hit at 6000 ft when pulling out of a dive. All three pilots spent more than five years in captivity. *MR BLACKBIRD* nose-art appeared on both sides of the aircraft.

11

F-105D-10-RE 60-0434 *DAMN YOU CHARLIE BROWN!* of the 44th TFS/388th TFW, Korat RTAFB, Thailand, Summer 1967
Strike cameras, ECM antennas and pods were standard on most F-105s by mid-1967. 60-0434 was one of fifteen Thunderchiefs officially shot down by MiG-21s, this jet being hit from behind by an 'Atoll' missile in an unexpected dive attack by two VPAF fighters on 9 October 1967. Maj James Clements was approaching his Quang Hein railway marshalling yard target at 15,000 ft when his fighter was hit, forcing him to eject into captivity.

12

F-105D-20-RE 61-0132 *HANOI SPECIAL* of the 34th TFS/388th TFW, Korat RTAFB, Thailand, 1968
1Lt David Waldrop III had joined the 34th TFS after 45 combat missions as a TDY pilot with the 355th TFW. He had flown a 12 July 1967 Paul Doumer Bridge mission as flight leader on his first 388th TFW combat sortie. Flying as 'Crossbow 02' on 23 August 1967 during an assault on the Yen Vien railway marshalling complex, his jet carrying six M117s, an AIM-9B, ECM pod and wing tanks, Waldrop successfully bombed his target and then felled a MiG-17 with cannon fire. There was evidence to suggest that he had downed a second MiG too, but this remained unconfirmed. 61-0132 was lost on 14 May 1968 when its pilot, Maj Seymour Bass, collided with his flight leader over Thailand and was killed.

13

F-105D-25-RE 60-0424 *MICKEY TITTY Chi* of the 34th TFS/388th TFW, Korat RTAFB, Thailand, early 1967
This jet was flown by Maj Ralph L Kuster as 'Hambone 02' on 3 June 1967 when the 388th TFS attacked the Bac Giang railway bridge. As the lead flight, Kuster's F-105s were first to run through the SAMs using the tight 'pod' formation required for effective deployment of ECM. They drew heavy AAA on an approach to the target, and Kuster used his gun-camera to record the weapons' positions. Departing the target, the F-105s encountered MiG-17s, and Kuster (later noted for his extravagant moustache) and Capt Larry Wiggins ('Hambone 03') both shot a fighter down. The aircraft was hit by AAA on 10 July 1967 and MiG killer Maj Maurice Seaver ejected safely.

14

F-105F-1-RE 63-8317 *HALF FAST* of the 357th TFS/355th TFW, Takhli RTAFB, Thailand, December 1967
The aircraft received the TCTO 1F-105-1133 avionics refit that upgraded it to early F-105G-1 standard. On 19 December 1967, Capt Philip Drew and Maj William Wheeler (as 'Otter 03') scored the final F-105 MiG kill of the war during an *Iron Hand* mission. Getting in behind two pursuing MiG-17s, they approached one of the VPAF jets in its blind spot and destroyed it with 20 mm cannon fire.

Subsequently nicknamed *Root Pack Rat*, the aircraft fell to 37 mm fire while attacking a Phu Qui SAM site on 30 September 1968. Pilot Capt Clifford Wayne Fieszel and EWO Maj Howard Horton Smith remain missing in action.

15

F-105G-1-RE 62-4436 *FAT FANNY* of the 333rd TFS/355th TFW, Takhli RTAFB, Thailand, December 1968
Upgraded from an F-105F to G-1 configuration, this aircraft was flown by Maj Don Kilgus and Capt Ted Lowry as part of the 'Firebird' *Iron Hand* force supporting the Son Tay prison rescue attempt on 20/21 November 1970. SAM site suppression was effective in protecting the strike force, but two of the 18 SAMs fired from eight sites hit F-105Gs. Kilgus' jet was holed in the fuel tank, forcing the crew to eject near the Plain of Jars, from where they were rescued by HH-53 helicopters. Another F-105G, 'Firebird 3', flown by Majs Everett Fansler and Bill Starkey, was damaged but recovered.

16

F-105D-30-RE 62-4270 of the 34th TFS/388th TFW, Korat RTAFB, Thailand, early 1969
Assigned to Col Garrett, this aircraft bore the cod-Latin motto *Noli Non Legitime Carbor Undum Est* ('Don't let the bastards grind you down') around its 'zonked tiger' nose-art. 62-4270 was hit by AAA when 1Lt R A Stafford made his fourth pass at a road target during a *Steel Tiger* mission on 29 March 1969. The pilot ejected from the burning aircraft and was rescued by a USAF helicopter.

17

F-105D-25-RE 61-0176 *The Jolly Roger* of the 357th TFS/355th TFW, Takhli RTAFB, Thailand, January 1970
Assigned to Maj R E Rogers, this aircraft is seen here with 2000-lb Mk 84 and 500-lb Mk 82 bombs and a replacement vented gun-bay door from a reverse-camouflaged aircraft. 61-0176 made its service debut with the 67th TFS/18th TFW at Kadena AB in November 1962, and it returned to the USA when transferred to the 4th TFW in August 1964. Remaining with the latter wing through to December 1965, it participated in a TDY to Takhli RTAFB with the 6441st TFW during this time. Transferring to the 23rd TFW, the aircraft eventually returned to the 18th TFW on 25 July 1966 as an attrition replacement for both 388th and 355th TFWs. It was passed on to the 354th TFS at Takhli on 1 November 1967, and the fighter remained here until the base closed in 1970. After eight years with the Kansas ANG's 184th TFTG, 61-0176 served with the AFRES's 457th and 466th TFSs, before being retired to the USAF Museum with 5813.1 flying hours to its name. In combat, the jet was hit just twice by single 12.7 mm bullets, requiring a mere two man-hours of repairs.

18

F-105D-20-RE 61-0159 *Honeypot II*/*HAVE GUN*

WILL TRAVEL **of the 354th TFS/355th TFW, Takhli RTAFB, Thailand, May 1967**
This aircraft retained its nicknames post-war when it served for eight years with the Virginia ANG. The 434th F-105 built, 61-0159 had entered service with the 36th TFW at Bitburg AB, in West Germany, in 1962, after which it flew for 18 months with the 4th TFW – including a spell in July 1965 with the 335th TFS TDY at Takhli as part of the 6441st TFW. On 18 February 1966 the jet was assigned to the 355th TFW, with whom it remained until October 1970. 61-0159 was battle-damaged several times during this period, including suffering a AAA hit to the centreline tank. When the pilot jettisoned the latter it damaged the aircraft's belly, tearing off part of the right stabilator. Although assigned to 1Lt Robert B Goodman in the spring of 1967, it was Capt Jacques A Suzanne who used it to down a MiG-17 on 12 May. In February 1970 it became the first F-105 to reach the type's 4000-hour design limit. The aircraft went on to accumulate another 2094 flying hours before it was placed in storage at Davis-Monthan AFB. The veteran Thunderchief was eventually put on display in the markings of Col Howard C 'Scrappy' Johnson, founder of the Red River Valley Fighter Pilots' Association, The River Rats.

19

F-105D-31-RE 62-4360 *IRON DUKE* of the 354th TFS/355th TFW, Takhli RTAFB, Thailand, May 1970
Delivered to the 8th TFW at Itazuke AB in August 1963, 62-4360 transferred to the 41st AD at Yokota AB in May 1964. It was then passed on to the 6441st TFW and thence to the 23rd TFW and TDY deployments with the 355th TFW. For most of 1966-67 62-4360 stood nuclear alert at Yokota AB, with a transfer to the 18th TFW at Kadena AB following in January 1968. From September of that year the jet was at Korat with the 388th TFW, where it gained the nicknames *12 O'Clock High* (469th TFS) and *Screaming Eagle* (44th TFS). Returning briefly to the 355th TFW in April 1970 (when it was assigned to 1Lt Allan V Shulke, who named it *IRON DUKE*), the F-105 had been transferred back to the 18th TFW by 10 October 1970. Here it remained until further reassignment to the AFRES's 507th TFG in May 1972. Following two years as an Aircraft Battle Damage Repair (ABDR) airframe at McClellan AFB in 1983-85, the jet was passed on to the USAF Museum for display at Tinker AFB.

20

F-105D-31-RE 62-4387 *HELL'S ANGEL*/*The Grim Reaper* of the 354th TFS/355th TFW, Takhli RTAFB, Thailand, May 1970
Originally delivered to the 8th TFW at Itazuke AB, Japan, 62-4387 served with the 41st AD and the 6441st TFW at Yokota AB, prior to transferring to the 388th TFW at Korat as *Eve of Destruction* (34th TFS). In November 1968 62-4387 was transferred to the 355th TFW, with whom it remained until October 1970 (the jet was assigned to 1Lt Chuck de

Vlaming for much of this time). Later, it served for 11 years with the Kansas ANG and AFRES units prior to being preserved at Lackland AFB.

21

F-105G-1-RE 63-8319 *Sinister Vampire* **of the 44th TFS/355th TFW, Takhli RTAFB, Thailand, 1970**
Originally with the 36th TFW, this jet later flew with the 561st TFS and 17th WWS prior to being transferred to the Georgia ANG. Updated to F-105G-1-RE configuration, it was variously nicknamed *SAM Seeker*, *Linda Jean*, *Tuffy* and *Hugger Mugger*. The aircraft saw post-war service with the Georgia ANG's 128th TFS before ending its days as a missile target on the Aberdeen Proving Grounds in Maryland.

22

F-105D-10-RE 60-5375 *OLD CROW II* **of the 33rd TFS/355th TFW, Takhli RTAFB, Thailand, 1970**
This aircraft is seen in the markings it wore whilst assigned to Col Clarence 'Bud' Anderson, CO of the 355th TFW (and a World War 2 fighter ace) from 22 June 1970 during the final stage of the wing's tenancy at Takhli. When the wing left on 10 December 1970, it completed a five-year deployment in which it had flown 101,304 combat sorties, delivered 202,596 tons of bombs, destroyed 12,675 targets and shot down 20 MiGs (plus eight destroyed on the ground) at a cost of 136 aircrew and 181 aircraft. This jet later flew with the 563rd TFS/23rd TFW until it was lost in a mid-air collision with 60-0513 in February 1974.

23

F-105D-5-RE 59-1731 *The Frito Bandito* **of the 357th TFS/355th TFW, Takhli RTAFB, Thailand 1970**
Previously with the 388th TFW, 59-1731 is depicted here as it looked when assigned to Maj Jose Olvera and armed with AGM-12C Bullpups. By 1980 it was serving with the Virginia ANG as *The Hun's Hammer*. After retirement to AMARC the fighter was sold at a scrap price in August 1996 to the Gateway Fighter and Aircraft Museum of St Louis, Missouri.

24

F-105G-1-RE 63-8311 *SAM FIGHTER* **of the 354th TFS/355th TFW, Takhli RTAFB, Thailand, 1970**
This jet was originally assigned to the USAFE-based 49th TFW, led by Col William Chairsell from August 1964 and Col John C Giraudo from 21 June 1966. The former subsequently moved to Korat to head up the 388th TFW, while Col Giraudo commanded the 355th TFW at Takhli from August 1967. 63-8311 was transferred to the 6010th WWS/388th TFW and crashed in Thailand after engine failure on 15 November 1970.

25

F-105G-1-RE 62-4439 *HOPELESS/Truckin' Mama* **of Det 1, 561st TFS/388th TFW, Korat RTAFB, Thailand, Summer 1972**

Assigned to Majs Dan Barry and John Forrester, this aircraft had a down-beat nickname that may have reflected the situation in Vietnam. However, as Dan Barry recalled, 'One of my superstitions about aeroplanes was I felt that they all had personalities, and I always avoided maligning them at all costs lest they take offence! I can only guess that maybe John and I ended up with our names on an aeroplane that had been assigned to someone else who called it *HOPELESS*'. Det 1 initially used the 23rd TFW base code (MD), but changed to WW with their new parent unit, the 832nd AD, in July 1972. 62-4439 finally ended its days as an Aberdeen Proving Grounds test target.

26

F-105G-1-RE 63-8266 *WHITE LIGHTNING* **of the 17th WWS/388th TFW, Korat RTAFB, Thailand, February 1973**
Transferred from the 561st TFS's Det 1 with the nickname *Can't Mack It To It*, this aircraft was initially accepted as an F-105F on 25 March 1964 for the 4520th CCTW at Nellis AFB. It continued in the training role with the 23rd TFW at McConnell AFB in 1966-67, and then with the 4525th FWW and, in October 1969, the 57th TFW back at Nellis AFB. Converted to F-105G-1-RE configuration by 3 March 1971, 63-8266 flew to Korat RTAFB for service with the 388th TFW until 7 September 1973, when it was reassigned to the 35th TFW. The aircraft was removed from AMARC storage in November 1990 for the Mid-America Air Museum of Liberal, Kansas.

27

F-105G-1-RE 62-4446 of the 17th WWS/388th TFW, Korat RTAFB, Thailand, March 1973
This aircraft is depicted here towards the end of a long combat career that had begun on 2 January 1967 as a 388th TFW *Commando Nail* ('Ryan's Raiders') F-105F. Delivered new to the 23rd TFW as a trainer in March 1964, it joined the Operation *One Buck Nine* deployment to the 6441st TFW at Yokota AB in May 1965. Back with the 23rd TFW in May 1965, 62-4446 then moved to Nellis AFB, prior to conducting a combat deployment to Korat RTAFB. Damaged during *Commando Nail* missions, it was 'de-modified' to standard F-105F configuration for 388th TFW service until October 1969. The jet then flew numerous 44th TFS *Iron Hand* missions in the *Steel Tiger* area, sustaining combat damage several times. It transferred with the 44th TFS to Takhli in October 1969, where the aircraft was field-modified to F-105G-1-RE configuration by SMAMA depot engineers. After crash damage repair at McClellan AFB, it returned to the 388th TFW until October 1974. Service with the 35th TFW at George AFB, California, followed, then a two-year ANG period ending in storage at AMARC in July 1982. In October 1984 the fighter was revived for use as an ABDR training airframe at Incirlik AB, in Turkey. It was then put on display at Spangdahlem AB, Germany, in 1988 as a memorial to Vietnam War PoW and MIA airmen.

INDEX